Philippe Quinault's Comedy
The Indiscreet Lover, or the Master Blunderer

Philippe Quinault's Comedy
The Indiscreet Lover,
or The Master Blunderer

TRANSLATED FROM THE FRENCH BY

Dr. Alexandra Kaminska
The University of Wisconsin-Stevens Point

With an Introduction
on the Historical Development of Comedy
and Theories About Comedy,
and with a Section Devoted to Methods
in Teaching Comparative Literature

An Exposition-University Book

EXPOSITION PRESS   HICKSVILLE, NEW YORK

To create mutual respect in the world, an addition to its common treasure of literature, for purposes of peaceful understanding among the nations and ethnic groups.

CONTENTS

ACKNOWLEDGMENTS

This work has been promoted by the kindness of Signora Giovanna Sciarrone of Stevens Point, Wisconsin, an Italian-born lady, who corrected my knowledge of Italian in translating Barbieri's *Inavvertito*. I wish to thank her for her help.

In addition, The Interlibrary Loan of the Learning Resources Center, University of Wisconsin-Stevens Point, has done a wonderful work in providing me with all the works I needed. I wish to express my gratitude and appreciation to Mrs. Kathleen Halsey, chief Interlibrary Loan Manager of the Learning Resources Center.

INTRODUCTION

I. EUROPEAN THEORIES: THE DIFFERENT CONCEPTS OF COMEDY THROUGHOUT THE AGES

Aristotle (384-322 B.C.) wrote his *Poetics*, which came down to our common treasure of literature only in parts. According to this Greek philosopher, the common feature of any literary genre is imitation, *mimesis*. Comedy is an imitation of bad characters, yet it does not imitate them according to every vice, but the ridiculous only, since the ridiculous is a part of turpitude. *For the ridiculous is a certain error, and turpitude unattended with pain, and not destructive.* For Aristotle the human being has an inherent motive power, the *mimesis*. This driving force has initiated every genre of poetry. It is the main principle of creativity. The main difference between tragedy and comedy is, according to Aristotle, the imitation of ridiculous, vile characters in comedy, while the imitation of tragedy deals with heroes, supermen. Aristotle planned a treatise about comedy in particular, but it never came down to us. Tragedy has to create a cleansing effect in the spectator, through compassion and fear. The Aristotelian concept of *catharsis* (purging) means a relief from lust.

From our contemporary point of view the consideration of Aristotle's *Poetics* has some insufficient notions: the differentiation between good and vile characters, which changes at different times, according to individual and ethnic ideals.

Ælius Donatus, who lived in the middle of the fourth century A.D., wrote about *Comedy and Tragedy*. A fragment of this work was included in all the early printed editions of Terence's works. Throughout the Middle Ages, Donatus was known and his work was accepted as the main theoretical manual about comedy

1

and tragedy, until Aristotle's work became known. In studying
Donatus we get acquainted with Horace, whom Donatus frequently quoted. Donatus is the last of the Latin theoretical writers
on comedy during the Middle Ages. The first printed edition of his
Commentaries on Terence, published at Cologne, 1470-72, con-
tained *De Comoedia et Tragoedia.* His ideas about comedy are:
comedy is a story treating various habits and customs of public
and private affairs, from which one may learn what is of use in life,
on the one hand, and what must be avoided, on the other hand.
Thus Donatus teaches that comedy has an educational goal.
Many comedy writers of the following centuries followed his advice, among others Molière.

In comparing Aristotle's *Poetics* with the *Comedy and Tragedy* by Donatus, we may find that Donatus added to the Aristotelian theory of imitation the idea of the educational value of
theatrical performances. Imitation of life led to realistic portrayals of the surrounding world, while educational concepts of
teaching through laughter led to the presentation of types, i.e.,
representatives of one virtue or of one vice in the theatre of the
seventeenth century, especially in France.

Horace (65-8 B.C.), in *De Arte Poetica (About Poetic Art),*
shows many subdivisions of comedy. It may be a barefoot comedy,
because of the low order of the plot and poorness of the players:
or it may be because these comedies are not concerned with the
affairs of people in towers or attics, but of the inhabitants of low,
humble places. He divides all comedies into four parts: the title
role, the scene of action, the situation, and the outcome. The
Prologue pronounces the first speech about events preceding the
action. The *Protasis* is the beginning of the dramatic action, part
of which is withheld for suspense. The *Epitasis* brings the further
development of the situation. The *Catastrophe* is the solution,
which is pleasant in a comedy.

Horace's concept of comedy emphasizes the social differ-
ences between humble and rich persons, gives the comedy a
strong structure, and refers to comedies under Greek inspiration,
where the actors wear Greek costumes, to comedies introducing
Roman habits and local affairs, where the actors wear Roman

costumes, and to comedies in which not the plot, but witticism is mainly emphasized.

Pierre Corneille, a celebrated French playwright of the seventeenth century, wrote in his *Premier Discours. De l'Utilité et des parties du poème dramatique* that comedy and tragedy resemble each other. The seventeenth century in France applied the word *comedy* even to tragedy if it was played by professional comedians. Madame de Sevigné wrote to her daughter that "this night a comedy of Racine is going to be played, *Phèdre.*" This play by Racine is considered the best model of a tragedy, according to Aristotelian rules. The French seventeenth-century pseudo-classic playwrights and the author of *L'Art poétique,* Boileau-Despréaux (1636-1711), mixed these notions of comedy and tragedy. His *L'Art poétique* (1674) is a kind of codification of previously existing rules about different literary genres. Song III of this work is devoted to tragedy and comedy, as well as to epic poems. Bolieau's basic point of view is his concept of reason, connected with Descartes's teaching. All that is shocking to human common sense has to be avoided. Reason facilitates the perception of truth, which is the first and main principle of beauty. Since truth appears mainly in nature, poetry should be based on the imitation of nature. Therefore, everything burlesque should be avoided. Boileau-Despréaux saw the implementation of his ideas in the Greek-Latin antiquity, criticizing his contemporaries. His *Poetic Art* became the point of departure of a dispute between the admirers of the antiquity and those who saw rather good qualities and progress in the modern poetry, the *Querelle des Anciens et des Modernes,* which lasted for about two hundred years in France, and, actually, never was finished.

English literary criticism, with regard to comedy and tragedy, is derived partly from the ancients, and partly from Italian scholars. William Congreve (1670-1729) is the master of the English comedy of manners. His remarks on the drama make his own works and those of his contemporaries appear in full light. Congreve uses the comparative method with regard to the plays of other ethnic group representatives. He maintains that English humor is "almost of English growth, at least, it does not seem to have found such increase on any other soil." And what appears to Congreve to be the reason of it is the greater freedom, privilege, and liberty which the common people of England enjoy.[1]

With regard to his own comic plays Congreve says, in the *Epistle Dedicatory to The Double Dealer:* "I designated the moral first, and to that moral I invented the fable."

If we consider that contemporary critics divide playwrights into those who teach through their theatrical performances and those who write only for amusement, Congreve belongs to the group of the so-called "engaged playwrights," i.e., he composes his plays with a preconceived idea of which his characters serve as illustration.

The Irish playwright George Farquhar (1677 or 1678-1707) published a little collection of miscellaneous prose and verse, in which he included his *Discourse upon Comedy.* This *Discourse* is an anticlassic rejection of the so-called Aristotelian Unities, which were misunderstood by the pseudo-classicists. The *Discourse* was published in 1702 and is only a light essay, but it brought into full light what other playwrights have practiced, the rejection of classical rules.[2] An interesting passage of Farquhar's theory is the following:

Aristotle was no poet, and consequently not capable of giving instructions in the art of poetry; his Ars poetica *are only some observations drawn from the works of Homer and Euripides, which may be mere accidents resulting casually from the composition of the works, and not any of the essential principles in which they are compiled.*

If we follow the theories concerning comedy according to the fact that some playwrights and theoreticians accepted the classical heritage and some did not, and agreed with the Moderns in the *Querelle des Anciens et des Modernes,* there remain very few, and those not the best, to accept the classical rules of the unities. The most remarkable rejection of the classical heritage is offered by the so-called antiplay, illustrated best by Ionesco.

Ionesco discards almost all conventional elements of the theatre: there is no plot; there are no characters in the conventional sense. Ionesco states that his plays are not high comedies but farces with the exaggeration of burlesque humor up to the paroxysm of tragedy. Original powerful comic qualities are juxtaposed with original powerful tragic elements.[3] Corresponding are the linguistic problems: antiintellectual, irrational, at the borderline of absurdity.

Both Farquhar and Ionesco broke with the traditional theories about playwriting not only in discourses about comedy, but in their comedies as well, where they present quite new techniques. Farquhar wrote *The Recruiting Officer*, a comedy in five acts, played for the first time in London, 1706, and *The Beaux' Stratagem*, played a year later, where the place of the dramatic action is not London, but the province, while former playwrights (to quote only Etherege, Wycherley, and Congreve) preferred London as place of action. He broke with the conventions of the comedy of manners as well.

II. CLASSICAL COMEDIES AND THEIR HERITAGE TO THE END OF THE SIXTEENTH CENTURY

The word *comedy* has had different meanings throughout the centuries, in all the parts of the world. The word is derived from *komos*, which in Greek meant festival, and *ados*, a singer in Greek. It is commonly accepted that the Greek comedy originated in fertility rites and ritual drama of agricultural life.[4]

European drama began in Athens, in the fifth century B.C. Its origins have been traced with some probability to religious dances. Religious dances may be found in primitive cultures, but Greece probably was the only cultural country that developed theatrical shows from her religious dances. Drama, in its vague meaning, includes both tragedy and comedy. Both were regularly produced in Greece, during winter festivals of the god Dionysos in Athens. Both tragedy and comedy used the chorus in the so-called Old Attic period of comedies. The chorus was a group of dancers and actors who wore masks and expressed some reflections on the action. During the fifth century B.C. the only poet who wrote comedies in Athens was Aristophanes. His thirteen comedies that came down to us present a kind of comedy based on literary caricatures and on criticism of personalities and institutions of Athens. They are full of farces and wit. These comedies of Aristophanes ridiculed drunkards, animals, and the doctor, who became a grotesque figure. The tendency to burlesque and caricature is one of the earliest talents displayed by European playwrights.

In primitive times, no distinction was made between tragedy and comedy. Their separation is relatively recent. In Old Attic comedies we find serious themes blended with frivolous elements of humor.

The New Attic comedy is represented by Menander. His works came down to us in fragments only. In comparing the comedies of Aristophanes and those of Menander, we may recognize the change completed at Menander's time, i.e., ca. 342-292 B.C. The chorus disappears; the intricacies of Menander's plots are intended to divert rather than to criticize. Not sex ritual but romantic love forms the subject matter of Menander's comedies. Religion becomes a matter of habit, politics a dangerous complication of man, and slavery is presented as the preponderant lot of humanity. Menander's comedy is a comedy of manners, with a happy ending. The lovers are united; everything is solved to the satisfaction of the public. While Aristophanes represents the reforming trend of comedy, where theatre serves teaching purposes, Menander represents the trend of serving amusement only. The Roman theatre and the later playwrights imitated Menander widely.

Medieval theatres of Western Europe, up to the second half of the sixteenth century, suffered a break in the development of the classical comedy. Dante's *Comedy*, later called by his editors *The Divine Comedy*, was termed "comedy" because it offered criticism of the author's own time.

England's *Short Title Catalog* (STC) for the sixteenth century offers a portrayal of many editions of Latin comedies, especially of Terence (190-159 B.C.) and of Plautus (254-184 B.C.). The Renaissance revived the classics. The Elizabethan plays and the Pre-Elizabethan plays, from *Ralph Roister-Doister* and *Gammer Gurton's Needle* up to Shakespeare, offer a mixture of tragedy and comedy, in the sense that scenes of great protagonists are followed by grotesque scenes, while comedies present sometimes death or imminent destruction. Even Shakespeare's *Hamlet* has grotesque scenes of the grave-diggers following serious and tragical events.

Spanish comedies of the sixteenth century, as well as the later seventeenth-century comedies, used the term *comedy* for any play to denote its full-length secular character. Calderon, Lope de Vega, and some other playwrights were very fond of originality and avoided imitations of the classics.

The Italians developed the *commedia dell'arte* based on mime and gestures.

The classical heritage in European comedies had a great impact on the structure of the plays, especially with regard to the five-act play, with a climax in dramatic tension approximately towards the end of the third act or beginning of the fourth act. Those playwrights who followed the Old Attic comedy of Aristophanes tried to teach through their plays, following the idea that laughter is the best educator; those who chose Menander's New Attic comedy to be followed as a model wrote comedies for amusement only. Menander was translated by Plautus. The Latin comedies of Plautus and those of Terence served for a long time as sources of inspiration and imitation.

There were revolts against imitation of the classics, such as *La Querelle des Anciens et des Modernes,* the Romanticism, Realism, Naturalism, and the Antiplay. After each revolt followed a return to the classical symmetry, culture of the dialogue rather than great movement on stage, and high style of the word. To such returns to the classics belong the comedies of Marivaux in France, partly those of Fredro in Poland, of Lessing in Germany, and some others. Great authors like originality and avoid any imitation. Irony, a known classical device in tragedy and comedy, meaning that the public knows more than the protagonist about himself, can be traced in Kleist's play, *The Broken Jar* (in German *Der Zerbrochene Krug*). European comedy does not include great themes like tragedy. The characters are petty, as in classical comedies; they are ridiculous and full of self-adulation, as in their classical models, but their dialogue is modern in the sense that each person speaks another language appropriate to the character. The dialogue is modern also in the sense that it serves relief purposes, interrupting a conversation that risks becoming serious.

III. COMIC PLAYS DURING THE MIDDLE AGES

Some historians and critics of the medieval drama recognize that the medieval drama developed out of a religious context. To such historians and critics belong Chambers and Young. Religious ritual was the drama of the early Middle Ages and had been ever since the decline of the classical theatre.[5]

The *Liber Officialis* shows that the Mass was consciously interpreted as drama during the ninth century. Karl Young's *Drama of the Medieval Church* encourages the reader to a reading secularization, with a complementary stress on comic farces. Using documentary facts, Young refers to an impulse towards increasing the worldly appeal of the plays through the comic element, not existing in Latin medieval plays; he discusses the problem of gradual development that leads directly to the problem of evolution. Professor John M. Manly emphasizes, in an article published in 1907, "Literary Forms and the New Theory of the Origin of Species," the outstanding authority of American scholars regarding the origin of species in medieval drama. His article had considerable consideration. It led to three lengthy essays in Darwinian criticism by John P. Hoskins of Princeton. It was quoted approvingly by P. S. Allen, George C. Taylor, H. S. Jones, and George R. Coffman. It is still a living problem today.[6]

As long as drama was considered an organism in continuous development from the *Quem queritis* to *Hamlet,* any labeling was sufficient. But a new process was formed when an established characteristic change was added to the original complex. Labeling may have a qualitative and temporary value. With regard to drama it may be considered important to label *comedy* and *tragedy* separately, comedy offering a gap between the classical Attic comedy and the medieval farces or *sotties*.[7]

Christianity was opposed to the medieval comic plays. The medieval world was very puritanical. Only fools could allow themselves jokes and folly. The farces and *sotties* were given in the form of interplays between serious religious performances, called *Mysteries*. These medieval comic plays may be regarded as fragments of forgotten pagan cults, an effect of the secularization of medieval thought.

Ernst Robert Curtius gives us a portrayal of the split between the fervent piety of the Middle Ages and gnosticism, the inner conflict for many priests, criticism of celibacy and monasticism, especially during the twelfth and thirteenth centuries. The secularization of medieval thought converted from the religious and sacred to lay thought. It converted the humble people, who did not understand the Latin instructions of the clergy, to ridiculing the persons who taught religion and the instructions as well. It brought, as a result, the composition of farces and *sotties*.[8] The *sotties* had to attract people to the serious religious plays at the beginning of the series of shows; the farces had to give people some amusement at the end of the series. The great era of the farces and *sotties* was the fifteenth and the first half of the sixteenth centuries. Some farces seem to continue the French *fabliaux* tradition, i.e., the tradition of narrative poems including dialogues, written and sung for amusement of crowds. Both French farces and *fabliaux* had a kind of nondidactic humor, not ridiculing a whole class of the society, but making fun of some private scenes.[9] In comparing the French farces and *sotties* with German dramatic comic plays called *Schwank* (plural *Schwänke*), and Polish and Czech comic short plays, we perceive the main difference: the German dramatic *Schwank* introduced a central figure, which connected several *Schwänke* destined to be played on one evening show; it was a kind of merry jest, either in rhyme or in prose, often filled with a coarse humor; some *Schwänke* even had an obscene humor, with or without a didactic message; the Czech medieval comic theatre introduced the dispute, a kind of dialogue with personalized characters, such as *The Dispute of Water with Wine;* towards the end of the fourteenth century appeared satires on classes, such as *Podkoni a řék;* the Czech religious Easter plays developed scenes with a grocery seller,

called Mastičkár; this grocery seller became in the German
Schwänke the popular *Quacksalber;* Polish adaptations of classical comedies, especially of Plautus, include a moral teaching, not
known to Plautus. *The Tripled,* adapted from Plautus by Jan
Ostroróg, appeared in 1597, in five acts. It portrays a rascal son,
a type of the biblical prodigal son. The comedy includes some
farcical elements, such as the *quiproquo,* i.e., a character is not
recognized, but considered a stranger. The Polish *Tripled* is a
comedy, not a short play like a French or German jest.[10]

Concluding, we may say that the Middle Ages developed a
special kind of humor, characterized by the well-known French
historian of French literature: *"Heureux le génie à qui il a été
donné d'exciter le gros rire! Heureux le spectateur qui se dilate
au théâtre! Le rire délicat, ce rire de l'esprit que provoque le
ridicule finement exprimé, laisse une arrière-pensée triste et
comme un arrière-goût d'amertume."* (How happy is the genius
who has the gift of exciting people to a strong laughter! How
happy is the spectator who gladdens his heart in the theatre!
Delicate laughter, this kind of spiritual laughter caused by finely
expressed mockeries, leaves the impression of a sad reflection
promoting an after-taste of bitterness.)[11]

IV. COMEDIES OF THE MOST OUTSTANDING
     FRENCH PLAYWRIGHTS, THE THREE M'S,
     MOLIÈRE, MARIVAUX, AND MUSSET; BEAU-
     MARCHAIS AND IONESCO

The three M's represent three centuries of French comedy,
Molière the seventeenth, Marivaux the eighteenth, and Musset
the nineteenth.

Molière's plays, called comedies, offer a great variety in technique; nevertheless, there is a certain unity due to the author's
knowledge of his public, his taste, and its demands, and psychological insight into human beings. The labeling of his works "comedies" is based on Molière's sense of humor, and on the temporary meaning of the word. Some of his comedies are actually
tragedies. *Georges Dandin* is a tragedy; nevertheless, it is called

comedy. The psychological study of human nature is as deep in his first comedy, *The Blunderer,* as in the great comedies of his mature age, *Le Misanthrope,* or others. The differentiation is based on technicality. He did not yet achieve a full development of his technical means in the first comedy, *The Blunderer,* where the *dénouement* (ending) does not result from the plot; it is added to the action like a *deus ex machina* (a god solving a tense situation in the last moment in an artificial manner). On the contrary, the plays of his mature age, such as *Le Misanthrope,* do not solve the situation at all; their *dénouement* is not a happy ending; it leaves to the imagination of the spectator the pleasure of creating the ending by himself, according to his own good will and creative mind. Thus the ending may become happy or unhappy, and the spectator is satisfied with his role of cooperation with the playwright, according to his own taste.

Molière's knowledge of the Parisian society and of the French provinces was a result of his life. Born in Paris, he traveled a great deal with his theatrical group, then came back to Paris, where he spent the rest of his life. His knowledge of the human being deepened with every year. Some contemporary disputes on the false interpretation of religious duties brought *Tartuffe;* disputes on his satirical interpretation of such duties motivated Molière to write a work with a more orthodox outlook on religion, *Don Juan.*

The types of comedies Molière added to the common treasure of world theatrical plays are: farces, where slapstick humor is achieved through falling, beating, and tricks played upon a ridiculous character, such as *The Miser;* the type of a deceived husband, *Georges Dandin; quiproquo* devices in *Les Précieuses ridicules,* and supernatural forces intervening for the purposes of punishment of the immoral atheist, as in *Don Juan;* and Italian-type comedies, based on pantomime, which were offered by the *commedia dell'arte.* Some characters who reappear in several comedies, like Sganarel, are portrayed as having some typical features, always true in any place, such as the cunning servant, easily vulnerable and proud, and the solitary buffoon, gullible and betrayed, modeled on the Italian Scaramouche, with his ridiculous gestures, whimsical moods and his shrill voice; *Les Fourberies de Scapin (Scapin's Knaveries)* reveals a traditional Italian character, made French by the author's skill. His typical features are repeated in *Le dépit amoureux (The Resentment in Love), L'Etourdi (The Blunderer),* in the character of Mascarille, who also appears in *Les Précieuses ridicules (The Ridiculous Girls with an Exaggerated Taste).* This traditional character of a servant holding all the threads of the plot in his hands reappears later in French comedies such as *Le Legataire universal,* by Regnard (1708), *Turcaret* by Lesage (1709), *Figaro's Marriage* and *Le Barbier de Seville,* by Beaumarchais (1775-1784), and others. In Polish comedies Alexander Fredro gave a similar role to the characters of his servants; some other plays, the Romanesque comedies, often composed by Molière with the collaboration of others, like *Psyche,* are elegant plays presenting a dialogue of distinguished people of the high society who speak a sophisticated language. Later Marivaux developed this kind of dialogue in his eighteenth-century comedies, a dialogue called "marivaudage." Princes or other aristocratic characters are attentive to ladies of the high society, and the ladies are insensible to their suffering; some of Molière's comedies are known as the classical, the great comedies in five acts, modeled on the five-act structure of the Attic *epeisodions.*[12] Molière's classicism in these great comedies consists of borrowed themes in some of them, the goal to instruct through laughter, and the unities. Molière wrote, in the Preface to *Tartuffe:* "Les plus beaux traits d'une sérieuse morale sont moins puissants, le plus souvent, que ceux de la satire, et rien ne reprend mieux la plupart des hommes que la peinture de leurs défauts. C'est une grande atteinte aux vices que de les exposer à la risée de tout le monde."[13]

Among the great comedies of Molière are *Le Misanthrope* (1666); *Le Tartuffe* (1667); *Le Bourgeois Gentilhomme* (1670); *Les Femmes Savantes* (1672), and some comedies of mixed inspiration, like *Le Malade imaginaire* (1673), and others. Beyond manners portrayed in most of his comedies, Molière depicts in his great comedies personalities, strong individuals which are also eternally true types found in every country at any time. His characters are vital and complex, shaded with great art. Molière's model, in these great comedies, was life itself. His contemporary critics insulted Molière for having presented in *Tartuffe* an offense to religion. Actually, Molière never insulted religion, but the falsely understood piety by hypocrites who concealed their possessiveness behind airs of piety. Common sense was the most outstanding good quality Molière appreciated. Thus his spokesmen, like Madame Jourdain and her maid in *Le Bourgeois Gentilhomme (The Would-Be Gentleman)*, Orgon's wife in *Tartuffe*, Clitandre and Ariste in *Les Femmes Savantes (The Learned Ladies)*, and the Misanthrope's friend, Philinte, as well as the maids and male servants in most of his comedies, are representatives of common sense, of reason preached by Descartes, a contemporary philosopher in the seventeenth century. All that sinned against common sense was subject to satire, and Molière depicted it in the form of opposed camps. The representatives of each camp are convinced of their rightness. Their false wisdom, exaggeration in putting on airs and speaking affectedly, hypocrisy, and lack of good education are depicted with humor and satire.

In his great comedies Molière has every character speak a language appropriate to his features, situation, and mood. In other plays the dialogue is not yet so developed as in the great comedies, but already in his *Etourdi (Blunderer)* some characters speak another language than the others; thus the technique of Molière's dialogue developed. Some words in each comedy have an affective value, depending on the situation. They express either a deep respect or a simulated respect, or a disdain, as in Act I, Scene 2 of the *Learned Ladies*.

Laughter is created by comical characters whose fixed ideas are ridiculed; a disproportion of violent anger running wild through one word pronounced by an unimportant character (Philaminte's servant); an accumulation of compliments contrasted with abuse; a contrast between an arrogant beginning and a humble end of a speech, and play on words as in farces.

The protagonist of *Le Bourgeois Gentilhomme* is a tragicomical character who may be juxtaposed in the gallery of heroic-comical adventurers in world literature, like *Don Quixote* by Cervantes, like the would-be knights in Wittenwiler's *Ring*, or many others. The *Tartuffe* title-hero found a counterpart in Lady Cockwood, a lecherous old woman who, like Tartuffe, constantly emphasizes her virtue, in Sir George Etherege's five-act comedy *She Would If She Could* (1668), possibly inspired by Molière's impostor.[14] Alceste, the *Misanthrope,* possibly inspired the two English characters, Stanford and Emilia, in Shadwell's *The Sullen Lovers* (1668, reedited in 1670). Many other comedies of Molière found their counterparts in English plays, either by anonymous authors or by those who admitted knowing some of Molière's plays.[15]

Molière chose for his comedies some themes from the Latin comedies of Plautus. If we consider that, at this time, taking themes or motifs was considered rather a good quality, and that plagiarism was an invention which is relatively recent, that authors were proud of having treated the same theme or motif as a famous playwright, our contemporary judgment should be revised, with regard to accusing authors of "stealing themes," being "influenced," and so on.

Marivaux (1688-1763), the author of many eighteenth-century comedies, represents the light conversational art of the Regency. His best-known comedies are *Double Inconstancy* (1728), *The False Confidences* (1737), and *The Game of Love and Chance* (1730). Compared with the paintings of his contemporaries, such as Watteau (1684-1721), Boucher (1703-1770), and Fragonard (1723-1803) as well as with the Rococo decorative art of this creative period, Marivaux's comedies portray people taking life easily. The style of his dialogue is ingenious, subtle, vivacious, courteous, using refined words if pronounced by some members of the high society, vulgar expressions in the mouth of servants and other middle-class people. The conversational style of his comedies was known as "marivaudage," a label created probably from Marivaux's name. Sainte-Beuve, a French critic of the nineteenth century, expressed the opinion that this word does not even recall Marivaux. It does not designate any trend or school in literature. It appeared in literature during Marivaux's time. We may accept this label as character-istic of the style of dialogues in a refined manner, having a moral analysis as central theme. Some contemporary French critics use this word to familiarize the public with American films presenting comedy.

The dialogue in Marivaux's comedies is concerned mainly with the love of young people. The avowal of love comes late. Marivaux is primarily interested in young ladies awakening to love like rose buds which are developing to open themselves. Molière's characters, with the exception of Agnes in *The School of Women*, already are in love. Marivaux never mentions any passionate feeling (such as appears in Racine's tragedies). He is known as the author of comedies portraying *l'amour naissant* (love in its originating stage). No social relationship is depicted seriously. Many realistic details serve to portray the psychological insight and the changes of tension in each comedy. There is a certain discrepancy between the roles the characters have to play, by their own choice, and their disguise, as in Arlequin and Lisette, in *The Game of Love and Chance*. Their personality is never caricatured. Some features of the male servant disguised as his master are borrowed from the Italian *commedia dell'arte*, for example, his literary excursion and his vulgar speech.

The light atmosphere without any moralizing intentions re-flects the prerevolutionary mood of the French society, under Louis XV.

With regard to the psychological insight in portrayals of his characters, Marivaux may be compared to Shakespeare, but the English master is more philosophical. Marivaux is interesting as the playwright portraying the young lady opening herself to love and life. His happy ending brings her to marriage. What happens then is left to the imagination of the public.

Musset (1810-1857) was a Parisian-born poet and playwright. Like other Parisians, Molière and Beaumarchais included, Alfred de Musset offered the kind of humor known as the Parisian hu-mor, full of wit and irony. He expressed also some serious ideas in his comedies.

Musset's comedies are numerous. Among the best-known are:

Fantasio, Camille and Perdican (in French *On ne badine pas avec l'amour*), *The Candelabrum*, a *Collection of Comedies and Proverbs*, full of charm and wit. Musset was a member of the French Academy. The characters depicted in his comedies are his self-portraits, such as Coelio and Octave in *Les Caprices de Marianne*, Perdican in *Camille and Perdican*, and Lorenzaccio in a play under this name. *Lorenzaccio* may be considered a serious drama, full of Shakespearean problems comparable to Hamlet's "to be or not to be," or others. Musset's comedies include, besides humor and irony, a romantic spleen, a disgust with life, a suffering for the evil of the world. His characters show a kind of introspection which, since Shakespeare, has been one of the most beloved and analyzed criteria of appreciation in literature. If we judge Musset's works from this point of view, they may be cited among those of the most celebrated dramatists of the world. We may recognize in Musset's comedies the portrayal of our own foolish youth and unsolved problems.

Musset's style has been new in its technique. His *Spectacle dans un fauteuil* is a collection of comedies written not to be played, but read in an armchair. After a failure with his *Nuit Vénitienne*, in 1831, the poet decided never to write again for the stage, but to write for reading purposes. Thus the stage effects show many difficulties, since the place changes constantly, from scene to scene. Published in 1832, they all renewed the technical part of performances. All of Musset's comedies are still in the repertoire of French theatres, and some in the repertoire of foreign theatres. The plot in Musset's comedies is not complicated. Musset does not use the slapstick kind of *quiproquo*, or disguise. The conversation of his characters is simple, natural, derived from Musset's own thoughts. The charm of his comedies lies in the atmosphere of young love in its manifold stages, and in the satire while portraying old tutors. The simplicity of Musset's scenes has been appreciated as a classical structure of his plays.

Among celebrated French playwrights, besides the three M's, are others who, like Beaumarchais or Ionesco, deserve full appreciation. Beaumarchais is known to the public through Mozart's and Rossini's operas rather than through his comedies. He gave to old themes a new meaning. His Figaro, a trickster, is a personality of the prerevolutionary period of France: he is self-dependent, a barber, was formerly a servant to Count Almaviva, and helps his former master as his friend, not as a former servant. The author suggests that in the future such personalities will be successful, and seems to believe that without their help all will go wrong.

Beaumarchais has a wonderful sense of humor and a brilliant fluent language. *The Barber of Seville,* by Beaumarchais, has a plot sharpened by social criticism, in a provocative manner. Good qualities of the society are contrasted with weaknesses and privileges of the nobility. The social satire is included in the angry monologue of Act V, Scene 3. The society is satirized, the nobility and aristocracy are ridiculed, justice mocked at. The most characteristic words pronounced by Figaro in this monologue are: "You have troubled yourself to be born, nothing else; you are, besides, nothing else." Figaro confronts the aristocratic privileges with his own talents and knowledge as the gifts of the proletarian man.

Beaumarchais protests, in his Preface to *Figaro's Marriage,* against any prudish commonplaces in the theatre and demands that playwrights not only amuse and censure the characters they depict, but that they depict the century as it is in reality. Social abuses desolate the society, and the playwright has to reserve his strokes for those abuses. Thus not only characters, but the evil that hurts the society should be depicted. Beaumarchais's goal is thus to give a political and social satire, especially directed against prejudice. In *Figaro's Marriage* he presents the marriage of a servant and opposes master and servant as rivals in love.

For the public Beaumarchais's humor is more important than his social satire. *Figaro's Marriage* offers a spiritual dialogue, an antiprejudice monologue, comical situations, and a rhythmical French language, which is lost in translation.

The three M's and Beaumarchais are internationally accepted great playwrights, but they all present in their comedies some national features, due to the French humor, wit, and irony.

Ionesco, originally Ionescu, son of a Rumanian father and a French mother, is a representative of an international movement, the antiplay, unlimited by national boundaries.

The authors of the antiplay flee from their country: Joyce leaves Ireland, refusing to serve what he no longer believes; Ibsen, the Norwegian, goes to Rome, later to Germany, declaring: "I had to flee the swinishness up there to feel fully cleansed." The Swedish Strindberg finds refuge in Paris from the real and imagined abuse of his countrymen. Shaw leaves Ireland forever to live in England. Brecht, in retreat from the Nazis, moves to Scandinavia and thence to the United States, and Genet spends most of his life in European jails. As result, the theatre presents the antiplay as a kind of revolt nourished by international sources. The playwright sometimes even continues to write his plays in his own country, but no longer exalts it or advances its cause.[16]

In the past, now and then there were some rejections of classical rules, but a deliberate demonstration against any rational explanations of life's problems and against metaphysical subject matter, not in words, but by portraying the absurdity of life, of our lack of communication in speaking, and by presenting a parody of human relationships appeared for the first time in the so-called antiplay.

Ionesco's antiplays depict the absurdity of life, of conversation, a destruction of human relationship.

Ionesco's antiplay *La Cantatrice Chauve*, in English translation *The Bald Soprano*, has been played in Paris for several years, every night, with the greatest success. Its first performance took place on a Parisian stage, in May 1950. The title has nothing in common with the action. It refers to a short remark, in the last scene but one, when a fireman asks Mrs. Smith: "What does the bald little girl do?" The answer is: "She still continues to have the same haircut." Before the play starts, the atmosphere is introduced by the author's directives about the scenery: "A good English home of the middle class, with English chairs. An English night talk. Mr. Smith, an Englishman in his English slippers, is sitting in an English armchair, smoking an English pipe, and reading an English newspaper, at an English fireplace. His eye-glasses are English, and he has a gray English teapot. Close to him his wife, an English lady, is knitting English socks, in an English armchair. A long English silence. The English clock strokes are heard . . . " The obtrusive repetition of the word "English" makes the impression of monotony; the couple has obviously nothing more to tell one another. This is a satire on nationalism. The following conversation is full of commonplace absurdities of estranged husband and wife, dull, and comical through this dullness. Mr. and Mrs. Martin arrive to visit the Smith family. While they wait for the hostess, they talk about the strange coincidence of having met already and having a daughter (the bald soprano). The spectator does not know whether this is a deliberate ironic acknowledgment of the fact that they really have forgotten their marriage and that their daughter has another parent, besides the one who speaks, or that the marriage is such an unimportant fact, of no consequence, that they feel overwhelmingly lonely.

The conversation between both couples, the Smiths and later the Martins, is a caricature of dialogue. Any subject matter becomes a kind of catching of a straw in a difficult situation. It seems that the participants catch it, but that it is unattainable. At some moments the conversation comes to a paroxysm of absurdities. Some words are pronounced without any coherence, in a chorus of alphabetic vowels, consonants, or some sounds like "ch, ch, ch," . . . "hm, hm, hm," which seem madly senseless and without any necessity.

The curtain falls and rises again, showing the starting scene. The difference, in the meeting of the Martins, is that this couple is no longer called Smith, as in the starting scene, but Martin, the younger generation of the Smiths. Through this fact Ionesco seems to say that the existence of the younger generation is equally dull, absurd, and meaningless.

Ionesco may have been inspired by some French farces and *sotties* of the Middle Ages. It is possible that the puppet theatre has been of importance in the creation of his "fantoches" (Italian *fantoccini*), i.e., acting persons without any personality, puppets moving on the string of the author's fancy. The comic world is brought to the border of tragedy, but this tragic world is not felt as such, since the puppetlike people are not aware of their intellectual and moral nothingness. No conscience, no morality, no feelings, an impossible nonsense brought to its utmost.

Some people reject Ionesco's antiplay in the conviction that it destroys everything.

Some philosophers accept Ionesco's absurdity as a parallel to the existentialist philosophy. For our purpose of comparative literature, the essential role of the antiplay, as represented by Ionesco, is its revolt against the traditional comedy of five acts and its rules of the unities, imposed by the pseudo-classical school.

V. SHAKESPEARE'S COMEDIES AND
JAMES JOYCE'S THEATRE OF REBELLION

The variety of Shakespeare's comedies, the various kinds of structure he employed offer to our judgment a large field of investigation. Shakespeare's subject matter is sometimes based on the classics, Plautus primarily. His *Comedy of Errors* is based on the *Menechmi* by Plautus. But Shakespeare changed the classical Prologue to an exposition in the first act, and the farcical scenes of Plautus to sentimental and lyrical scenes. He also introduced some comical elements, for example, the twin servants who attend twin heroes.

The Italian *commedia dell'arte* served Shakespeare to create his established character types and unsophisticated farcical interludes, for example in *The Taming of the Shrew*. In each play Shakespeare modified the conclusion, bringing his characters of several plots into a relation with each other. If Molière's comedies do not have a definite dénouement, leaving it to the imagination of the spectator, Shakespeare's comedies show a marked tendency toward a comprehensive dénouement. The final scenes of his comedies leave no doubt with regard to future development and bring the multiple plots together.

Life offers both tragical and comical moments, and plays that imitate life blend tragical and comical moments as well. In comedies, noble passion or emotion is suppressed. Causes are ignored, in order to create humor. Whether we consider Shakespeare's or modern vanguard comedies, there are appearances of truth only, not truth itself. If you want to laugh don't ask why. Reasons and further effects of the appearances of truth shown on stage may lead to a tragic dénouement.

Shakespeare was a philosopher, looking for the sympathy of the spectator. Where sympathy enters, laughter is excluded. Therefore, his comedies produce rather smiles than laughter.

There is a great deal of interpretive criticism of Shakespeare's comedies. In all Shakespearean comedies, with the exception of *Pericles*, civilization or art is contrasted with natural life, a modern theme which, in French literature, led to the main philosophy of Jean-Jacques Rousseau.

John Russell Brown, in his *Shakespeare and His Comedies*, considers *The Winter's Tale* as the most consistently concerned with love and friendship. Written in 1610, it is widely considered to be a complete artistic success. In a little over thirty lines Shakespeare outlined an emotional and intellectual world previously portrayed in whole plays. The truth is disguised rather than unmasked. The essential difference between *The Winter's Tale* and former comedies is found in the portrayal of the society. The members of the society are subtly involved with each other; they hide and pretend, are familiar with ideals and imperfections, feel momentary regrets for a lost innocence or take momentary comfort in a new generation. The aspect of the society is more conscious of imperfections; its members doubt the truth of the words and actions of others.[17] Leontes doubts Hermione's words and actions. The technical devices of *The Winter's Tale* are more effective than those of the former comedies through moments of silence followed by a sudden return of speech. This device connects Shakespeare's comedy *The Winter's Tale* with some modern plays, such as Wagner's opera *Tristan and Isolde* and Maeterlinck's symbolic drama. Maeterlinck wrote an essay on the value of silence in his collection of essays, *La Beauté intérieure*.

Shakespeare's comedy *The Winter's Tale* was misunderstood for several centuries. Recently, it is appreciated as the comedy that best expresses Shakespeare's manner of depicting the action.

From Shakespeare's comedies to Joyce's *Exiles,* through Ibsen's dramas, some development may be observed. The main features of the Shakespearean drama, as expressed in *The Winter's Tale,* as well as the role of religion ascribed to Catholicism in this comedy, may be compared to Joyce's *Exiles,* written in 1914, published in 1918.

The central theme of Joyce's play is the exile chosen by an artist who cannot stand any limitation of his artistic genius by Catholicism, the family, and Irish nationalism. The rebellion of the artist, Richard Rowan, lasted for eight years, until he decided to return to his home country with his wife and child. A friend, Robert Hand, tries to help him in finding a job. Hand falls in love with Rowan's wife; Hand's cousin, Beatrice, with Rowan. Rowan's wife, Bertha, is jealous and suspects Beatrice's intelligence to be a serious menace in winning Rowan's attention, because of her own lack of education. Both couples have to overcome a crisis. Finally, Rowan, who had tormented himself for a long time, acknowledges that only his wife can be of help to him, the rebel, and Bertha asks him to return to religion in full, since she is aware that only through this reacceptance of religion may she remain loyal to herself, and to him.

Since the sixteenth century, the fairy tale has been lost, but the essential theme of religion and its value for rehabilitation is developed and renewed. As in Ibsen's dramas, we find in *Exiles* an honest settlement with the past, with religion and their value.

Joyce's work is not a comedy, but this label has been lost in recent years. Instead, *drama* in its large meaning, including life's features entirely, with humor and tragedy, both interwoven in an ingenious manner, appears to be a more adequate label to designate plays of the turn of the nineteenth and twentieth centuries.

VI. SPANISH COMEDIES OF THE GOLDEN AGE OF SPAIN

In the development of the Spanish literary trends in comedies of the fifteenth through the seventeenth centuries, the tragicomedy about Calisto and Melibea, probably composed by Fernando de Rojas, published in 1499, played the most important role. The first edition of this work was published anonymously and without a title. At Seville, in 1501, appeared the first known edition, entitled *Comedia de Calisto y Melibea.* In an anagram the name of the author is indicated as Fernando Rojas. This tragicomedy[18] is mentioned in the history of literature as *La Celestina.* Up to the present, eighty editions have appeared in Spanish, and numerous others in other European languages. The subject matter is simple and not important. The work is in prose, with realistically presented characters, customs and habits of the Spanish society, analysis of feelings, and differentiation of the language. In their dramatic life the characters anticipate Shakespeare. Celestina, an old pandering woman, has become one of the best-known Spanish symbols in literature, next to Segismundo, appearing in Calderon's *La vida es sueño (Life is a Dream), The Cid, Don Quijote,* and so on. *La Celestina* marks the turn of the centuries, from the Middle Ages to the Renaissance. In this work sins are punished by death, but not as in Dante's *Divine Comedy,* where the punishment is a moralizing example for living people. The characters in *La Celestina* move without any moralizing standard. Rojas presents a kind of glorification of life itself, with a pessimistic view. This glorification of life is a well-known Renaissance motif, in the fine arts, in Shakespeare's works, and in the language of European countries which created neologisms (in France the program of *The Pléiade*). *La Celestina* is a synthesis of life experience and literary tradition accepted from Plautus, Terence, and others. The author must have known the medieval codes of love, the poems of the French troubadours, the romances of German knights, the legend of *Tristan and Iseut,* and others.

La Celestina, known as tragicomedy, is actually a work between a romance and a drama, but its role was to trace the direction in which the future Spanish theatre had to develop. The realism of its portrayals of people in different situations, the introspection regarding human feelings, the use of popular songs, legends, myth, were inspired by this work. For the first time the

Spanish language achieved its mature stage of development in *La Celestina*. All these features were of great importance in Lope de Vega's creativity.

Lope de Vega (Felix), who lived between 1562 and 1635, tried to transform the tragicomedy into a new kind of drama. Like Molière, he was an actor, director of a traveling theatre, and as such, he became acquainted with the needs of the public, its taste, and the kinds of amusement fitting this taste. He tried, therefore, to intersperse serious shows with short dialogue scenes, full of humorous situations. In this way the famous *pasos* of Lope de Vega and the *entremesas* of Cervantes were composed.

These short plays started a new Spanish dramatic genre, called *entremés*, in English *interludes*, in Italian *intermezzi*. The best known are the *intermés* plays by Cervantes. In 1615 eight of them were published, preceded by a short Prologue, where Cervantes states that as a playwright he developed the *pasos* of Rueda into the genre of *Intermés*. Besides, Cervantes states that his follower, Lope de Vega, is a marvelous creature of Nature who reigns over the Spanish stage. Nevertheless, it is Cervantes who created a literary genre which is most outstanding and deserves research.

Cervantes transformed the short French farce, which had a primitive form, into a comedy full of satire, humor similar to that of *Don Quixote*, and dynamic rhythm.

Lope de Vega was inspired by these *intermés* when he created a model of comedy for the entire Golden Age of the Spanish theatre. He wrote approximately 1,800 plays, one every week, for forty years. In his forty-seventh year (1609), Lope published a poem entitled *Arte nuevo de hacer comedias en este tiempo* ("About the new art of writing comedies in our time"), with the dedication to the Court Academy. Some parts are explicitly directed against the classical heritage. Lope de Vega declares there that in writing a comedy he locks up all rules on six keys, throws away Plautus and Terence, and tries to write a play which would strongly affect everybody in his feelings. He reduces the comedy from five to three acts; each has a special function in the structure of the play. Thus Lope de Vega created a model of three-act comedies which was influential up to our time. He demanded from poetry spontaneity issuing from a natural inspiration. He recommended blending comical with tragical elements for the portrayal of truth. The characters should speak a language corresponding to their special position. From classical units Lope de Vega accepted the unit of action, i.e., he excluded episodic digressions.

To a certain degree his comedy is a continuation of the Italian *commedia dell'arte,* since it creates a series of scenes spontaneously growing, taken from life, full of gesture, mimicry, movement, and words being fragments of the observed reality.

The characters portrayed in Vega's comedies do not offer psychological analysis, like French comedies; they are not developing, but the spectator may distinguish them through their action, which is presented like a flash of light, in critical moments and in sudden violent decisions. Through this fact the public takes an active role, since the playwright has everybody among the public make conclusions, not offering ready-made characteristics.[19]

Lope de Vega found many critics, especially in France, in spite of the fact that many playwrights there were inspired by his creativity.

A turn in the appreciation of Lope de Vega's characters in his comedies may be found in the classification of recurrent personalities, such as the *gracioso,* the witty servant accompanying his master, not cliché-like, as he was presented in comedies by Plautus, Terence, and later playwrights, but portrayed from life; the *alcahueta,* a reincarnation of *Celestina;* the *galan* (lover), a king, a father or an old man, a pretty lady entirely devoted to love, the *caballero* (a gentleman of noble origin), whose main features are jealousy and honor, bravery and courage. This classification was done by many critics, among them a group of candidates for a diploma of the University of California, under the direction of Professor Griswold Morley.

The action is in the hands of the *caballero,* who decides controversies with his sword in hand, and by his witty cunning servant, the *gracioso.* From this fact is derived the name of the Spanish comedy created by Lope de Vega, i.e., *comedia de capa y espada* (the comedy of cloak and sword). The *gracioso* reminds us of Molière's servants in many regards. He accepts gifts, is cunning, possessive, and a coward, but is the representative of common sense. The lover has many features of the knights of some medieval romances.

The ending of the comedy is usually a formula, a final request to be lenient in the appreciation of the comedy. Its spokesman is the *gracioso,* and his request is addressed to the public and to other authors.

There are sometimes situations in Vega's comedies which find some parallels in the paintings of Velázquez, especially with regard to the technical device of contrasted figures. A comparison may be made between *The Courtly Women,* by Velázquez, and some scenes which seem to be presented like animated pictures.

El Perro del Hortellano (The Gardner's Dog), composed in 1613, takes a Spanish proverb as starting point. The technical device used here became a beloved French game of the *salons de Paris,* during the seventeenth, eighteenth, and nineteenth centuries: a proverb becomes a comedy through improvisation of witty guests taking part in the game. Alfred de Musset created a whole series of such *comédies-proverbes,* during the first half of the nineteenth century.

VII. POLISH CLASSICAL COMEDIES
BY ALEXANDER FREDRO

Alexander Fredro (1793-1876) created in his comedies a portrayal of the Polish *szlachta* (nobility), giving to its representatives characteristic names that make them typical for one feature only, such as Raptusiewicz ("The Impetuous") and Milczek ("The Silent") in *Zemsta (The Vengeance),* a comedy in four acts, composed in 1834; or making some of his main characters symbolical for the relationship between husband and wife, as in the comedy in three acts entitled *Husband and Wife,* played for the first time in Lwów (Lemberg), in 1822; or satirizing the oath of celibacy made by young girls in a comedy in five acts, under the title *Śluby panieńskie (The Young Girls' Oath, or The*

Magnetic Force of Hearts), played for the first time in Lwów, in 1833.

Fredro was aware of the moral decline among the Polish nobility, during the first half of the nineteenth century. The *szlachta* fought, in a violent opposition, against the growing middle class, and were opposed to their social and economic development, unreasonably determined to have their own style continued, a style imitated from foreign models. Fredro's satire and irony point out, in a patriotic effort to improve what is wrong, the rotten morale within the *szlachta*. Thus his *Husband and Wife* lead some love affairs, lying to each other, and, as the title indicates, being representatives of any husband and any wife; a false friend and a maid are involved in the love affairs. The husband and wife become reconciled, but the other couple must go. In this way justice is accomplished: those who legally belong to each other remain together; the others have to leave, with a slight hope that they may, sometime in future, return and be friends again.

The theme of the moral decline of the Polish *szlachta* was in the center of interest among Polish comedy writers. It was developed by other Polish playwrights such as Wojciech Boguslawski (1757-1829) and Fryderyk Skarbek (1792-1866). Fredro's witty dialogue and his knowledge of stage-effective devices make his comedies more celebrated by the public and critics. *Husband and Wife* restores the ageless theme of the hoodwinker who is hoodwinked. Since the French farce *Le Garçon et l'Aveugle* (possibly 1266 or 1282) the humorous motif of the tricked trickster appeared in many European comedies. It portrays the tricksters in love affairs outwitted by the others in a way that proves the author's goals to raise the morale of the public, through a satire of a rotten married couple in *The Husband and Wife*.

A more Romantic love is shown in Fredro's comedy *Śluby panieńskie czyli Magnetyzm serca*, in verse, in the last version, after the first, six years before, in prose.

Fredro did not follow any literary school. He lived during the periods of Romanticism, the Polish Enlightenment, and Realism, in its beginning stage. He tried to portray life itself. He owes much to Molière, but, like Molière, he was more self-dependent than a follower of classical rules. If we speak of Fredro's classical comedies it is understood that "classical" comedies mean comedies being models of the highest class, having an established value in Polish literature, and distinguished from popular. Many of his comedies do not follow the five-act structure of classical or pseudo-classical plays, and he did not imitate the Greek or Roman comedies. Many features of his comedy *Šluby panieńskie* are autobiographical. Fredro had to fight for his wife until she could marry him.

The types of Fredro's comedy are decidedly marriage-oriented. Their humor and the comical situations, the light and differentiated dialogues full of coined words (neologisms) and proverbs make his plays models of comedy, teaching through laughter.

Fredro's comedies were preceded by three centuries of Polish theatre. The sixteenth-century dialogues of the Polish theatre differ from Western farces, *sotties, intermés,* and so on, through the social background, tending to teach through the theatre. While the Western medieval plays were composed for laughter only, Polish accents were educational. Thus we may range the Polish comic theatre among the *engaged* plays, as modern critics do, distinguishing *engaged* writings from art for art's sake.

The Polish *Judgment of Paris,* and *The Beggar's Tragedy,* in Polish *Sad Parysa, Tragedia żebracza* were translated into many languages and achieved three Czech editions in translation. They revealed the truth of everyday life in the sixteenth century. Composed and edited anonymously, they may be ranged among the English and German beggar operas and comedies.

An interesting eighteenth-century comedy on Copernicus was written in Poland by the Dutch humanist Gnaphaeus, entitled *Morosophus.* The author lived in Elbląg and was a teacher. His comedy was preceded by a pantomime which showed a parody on Copernicus, who lived at this time in Frombork and was the target of a Protestant attack for his Catholicism. This comedy has a message: scholars should not be haughty and inaccessible.

During the seventeenth century Mikolaj Rej (Nicolaus Rej) wrote a modern comedy in Polish, with characters based on living personalities.

The Sowizdjal-comedies written for the Polish comic theatre (in German translation they were called *Till Eulenspiegel* comedies) were usually played at court; therefore, they were called *Court Comedies.*[20]

VIII. THREE RUSSIAN PLAYWRIGHTS, GOGOL, CHEKHOV, AND TURGENEV

Gogol's *Inspector General* (*Revizor,* in Russian) was first produced in April 1836. A year before, Gogol asked his friend Pushkin to give him a theme for a comedy. Pushkin gave him an anecdote of his own life, in Nizhnyj Novgorod, where he was welcomed as an inspector general traveling incognito. The motif of a fake inspector general was taken from life and portrayed in a realistic humorous manner in Gogol's comedy.

In this theme Gogol's sense of humor and his ability to take notice of everything that was ridiculous in Czarist Russia found a rich field for a grotesque mockery. The mayor of a little Russian provincial town receives information that an inspector general is traveling incognito with secret instructions, and that this man will soon arrive in town. The employees of this town are scared. From this fact then are derived scenes of disorder, stupidity, and lack of responsibility among the employees. A young man arrives at an inn. He is starving, does not know how to pay his growing bills in the inn, and accepts invitations of the town administrative employees with surprise and stupid speeches.

The dialogue between the young man and the mayor of the town is one of the examples of the Russian technical device of parallel speaking: Khlestyakov, the fake inspector general, is afraid that the mayor may send him to jail for unpaid bills at the inn, while the mayor is afraid that the inspector general may find disorder in the administration. Both speak as if caught in a magic circle of their anxiety. They are, therefore, unable to understand what the other interlocutor says and wants.

Invited by the mayor to a party, Khlestyakov speaks in his silly manner, and his humbug is admired by the ladies of the mayor's house as witticism pronounced by a courteous young man. He does not understand the situation at all. The employees bring him gifts to bribe him. He accepts the gifts, becomes the bridegroom of the mayor's daughter, and escapes suddenly. After his departure, the arrival of the actual inspector general is announced. The guests remain terrified in a final animated picture.

Gogol is original in creating a comedy without the traditional love plot. Love is mentioned in a kind of parody of the traditional lovers in comedies. The fake inspector general is engaged to the mayor's daughter, but not through love. It is one of the many forms of bribery ridiculed by the author. This comedy has been created not to teach, but for the purposes of laughter only. The beginning and the end of the comedy have a parallel situation: the petty townspeople meeting in the mayor's house. The fact of parallel beginnings and endings of comedies may be considered as characteristic for the genre of frame comedies.

Chekhov's plays blend serious and comical scenes, like many others in the European theatre of the nineteenth century. *The Cherry Orchard (Vishnevyj Sad)* was composed 1901-1904, played by the Moscow Art Theatre, and published by the author as a "comedy." The comic element of this play is based on a satire with regard to the dispossessed people, on the lack of understanding between the members of different groups of the Russian society, and on the parallel talking in a kind of monologue in the presence of others. The servants imitate the manners of their bosses, and the members of the upper-class society criticize the world of today. This world is portrayed satirically as something replacing the old order and its values, without sentimental regrets.

The portrayal of the characters and their conversation reminds spectators of the impressionistic technique of painting: glimpses are given showing a kind of a spiritual snapshot of a situation, of a conversation, of a thought, and of its changes. These glimpses seem to conceal an ironic smile of the objective author, who remains neutral toward the class struggle in Russia, alternating between two sides of the society, as if he were an idle spectator watching his puppets move on a string, dangled from his own hands.

Turgenev's *A Month in the Country (Mesyats v Derevne)* had an interesting evolution: It was first performed in Moscow in January 1872, under this title. Its first version, *The Student,* was composed in Paris, 1848-1850. The subject and conception of the later versions are already fully developed in this first composition. Turgenev's goal was to present the idle *do-little* of the Russian commoners and the *unnecessary man.* This goal was more clearly shown in the first version than in the others. It is possible that Turgenev was inspired by the comedy of Honoré de Balzac, *La Marâtre (The Stepmother),* that was played in Paris in 1848, while Turgenev was in Paris. The second version of this comedy, *Two Women (Dve zhenshchyny),* was written in 1850. Both versions were forbidden by the czarist censor for many years. Turgenev felt compelled to change the social criticism of his play to a psychological theme and to conceal in this manner his satire. Finally, the comedy appeared in the progressive journal *Sovremennik (The Contemporary Companion),* in 1855. The Russian critics praised the linguistic and stylistic good qualities only, and were strongly opposed to its dramatic features. Turgenev had to state in a special Note of the first publication that this comedy had never been written for theatrical performances. Nevertheless, the play was shown in the Moscow Little Theatre in 1872, and was a failure. It was not until 1879 that the final version succeeded, in Petersburg. *A Month in the Country* is now evaluated as a forerunner to Chekhov's plays.

The *unnecessary man* is Rakitin, a friend of the family Islaev. He decides to escape the plotting members of the family and goes with a young man, the student Belyaev, to Moscow. This student did not notice that the female members of the family Islaev fell in love with him. Belyaev is the representative of common sense among the people living in a distant Russian provincial farmhouse, seriously passionate. Rakitin is a man of high culture, but shy. He loves the thirty-year-old wife of the landlord, Islaev, who tries to get rid of him. He is totally unnecessary to her, to the family, and represents any unnecessary man in the society. The last version of this comedy constitutes an important addition to the psychological comedy in Russia.

CONCLUSIONS

The variety of comedies and their structure as offered by European comedies lead to the following conclusions:

1. Theatre, including comedy, originated from the religious cult in pagan antiquity and during Christian activities of religious services, in a slow evolution. It sometimes took spontaneous forms, especially if it portrayed mockeries of the common man in interludes *(intermés)*, between serious plays, in farces, *sotties*, and then in comedies, during the Middle Ages and the first half of the sixteenth century.
2. While tragedy writing had a certain continuity and a dignity that never was questioned, comedy offered a variety of pro- and antitheories and plays. The Old Attic comedy with a chorus was replaced by the New Attic Comedy, without a chorus; medieval comic plays in France, Germany, and Spain, were replaced by comedies more or less imitating the classics. The imitation of the classics was reduced to the plot accepted from them and/or by the structure of the five-act comedies. The revolt against the imitation of the classics led to the *Querelle des Anciens et des Modernes,* which in France lasted for two centuries, and to the Romantic School, which introduced a revolt against all rules binding the poet, in all European countries. Nevertheless, some outstanding playwrights, like Alfred de Musset, included both classic and romantic elements in their comedies. The Romanticists were followed by the Theatre of Revolt, which created the antiplay. In this way, the ancient genre of comedy had a dramatic evolution, especially with regard to the pro- and anticlassical rules. Great comedy writers, like Shakespeare, Lope de Vega, Molière, and others, were no imitators. They depicted life from life itself. They added to the common treasure of literature new elements, like the *gracioso,* the *unnecessary man,* and so forth.

3. The classical heritage is very limited. The classical admirers introduced *(a)* the five-act structure, *(b)* the action led by servants, *(c)* comical elements of a rather external humor of words, situations, and types, not personalities. "Being in love" is understood as a permanent modifier included in the list of characters as "lover of. . . . "

4. The new nonclassical elements include the beginning of love that does not exist in the first act of the comedies; a new language, the *marivaudage;* personalities instead of universal types, and the inspiration comes more from medieval short plays, from *fabliaux,* farces, and other comic shows than from the Attic comedy.

5. If we intend to have a picture of the repertoire of European comedy actually still played we state that the comedies of those writers who were not following the classics or borrowed very little from them are still on the list. Shakespeare, Molière, Lope de Vega, the great Russians, Ionesco, and many others still hold the interest of the public. On the contrary, Racine, the greatest admirer of the classics, is read in schools, not played by the *Comédie Française,* with the exception of his religious plays performed on stage at Lenten time only. Other imitators of the classics had to adjust their plays to the taste of the public, i.e., to make some changes in customs and habits in actualizing them to the national character of their home country. Personal inspiration and portrayal of people modeled on life are always more interesting than imitation of foreign habits. The human spirit modifies the expression and understanding of life. Consequently, there is a philosophy of literary appreciation, depending on the sensibility of the public. In the development of this sensibility lies the germ of evolution.

The appreciation of foreign tastes and values leads to a mutual understanding of life, philosophy, and arts, as expressed by other than one's own ethnic group, and, on a larger scale, to peace.

NOTES

1. For more, see Congreve's prefaces and dedications to his plays.
2. No great playwright accepted fully the classical rules. Cf. the paragraphs on Shakespeare, Molière, the Spanish comedy writers, and others.
3. See Ionesco's "Notes" to his play *Les Chaises*.
4. Cf. Francis Macdonald Cornford, *The Origin of Attic Comedy* (Cambridge: UP, 1934), and James K. Feibleman, *In Praise of Comedy* (New York: Horizon Press, 1970).
5. See E. K. Chambers, *The Medieval Stage* (London: Oxford Press, 1903); and Karl Young, "Concerning the Origin of the Miracle Play," in *Manly Anniversary Studies in Language and Literature* (Chicago, 1923).
6. See H. H. Clark, "The Influence of Darwin on American Criticism," in *The Impact of Darwinian Thought on American Life and Culture* (Austin, Texas, 1959), pp. 27-36.
7. *Sotties* were a kind of farces played by organized societies of "fools" (French *sot* means fool) in comical colorful clothes. They often used political allusions to contemporaries and were allowed to say everything to the highest authorities. The *sotties* differed from farces through the quantity of characters. Farces introduced three or four characters, rarely more. Sotties had many characters. The order of medieval plays had *sotties* at the beginning, farces at the end of a series of plays.
8. For more see: Ernst Robert Curtius, *European Literature and the Latin Middle Ages*, Harper Torchbooks (New York and Evanston, 1953), pp. 119-124.
9. See also Barbara Bowen, *Les Caractéristiques essentielles de la farce française et leur survivance dans les années 1550-1620*, Illinois Studies in L. & L., 53 (Urbana: UI Press, 1964), pp. 1-9; and Emile Picot, *Recueil général des sotties*, SATF (Paris: Didot, 1902), p. xii.

10. A collection of German *Schwänke* may be found in Adalbert von Keller's *Fastnachtspiele aus dem fünfzehnten Jahrhundert*, Bibliothek des literarischen Vereins Stuttgart, 28 (Stuttgart, 1853). Excellent analyses of some German dramatic *Schwänke* are offered by Eckehard Catholy, in his work *Das Fastnachtspiel des Spätmittelalters, Gestalt und Funktion* (Tübingen: Niemayer, 1961).

11. Désiré Nisard, *Précis de l'Histoire de la littérature française* (Paris: Didot, 1878.)

12. The classic play was mainly divided into *Prologos, Epeisodion, Stasimon,* and *Epilogos.* The *Prologos* and *Epilogos* were represented by an impersonated character who introduced or gave the final remarks to the public about events that preceded or followed the action shown on the stage. The *Epeisodion* presented the action, the *Stasimon* the reflections or feelings of the Chorus.

13. "The most beautiful features of a seriously presented moral philosophy are less influential than a satire, and nothing mends better most of the people than a funny portrayal of their bad qualities. A great attack on vices consists in exposing them to the ridicule of everybody."

14. Two years after his composition of *She Would If She Could,* Etherege recommended the translation of *Molière's Tartuffe* to Melbourne.

15. Cf. André de Mandach, *Molière et la comédie de moeurs en Angleterre* (Neuchâtel: A la baconnière, 1946).

16. For more read Robert Brustein, *The Theatre of Revolt, Studies in Ibsen, Strindberg, Chekhov, Brecht, Pirandello, Shaw,* ... An Atlantic Monthly Press Book (Boston: Little, 1964), p. 10ff.

17. John Russell Brown, *Shakespeare and His Comedies* (London: Methuen, 1968, rpt. from 1957), pp. 209-235.

18. *Tragicomedy* meant first a play where the gods and kings were involved in comical adventures. In the sixteenth century, in Italy, the tragicomedy meant a play presenting tragical events, but ending well, or a tragedy where comical

and tragical elements are interspersed. The Spanish tragicomedy has sentimental features mixed with tragical events
and with a happy ending.

19. Cf. Ernest Martinenche, *La comédie espagnole en France,
de Hardy à Racine* (Paris, 1900), and Morel-Fatio, *L'arte
nuevo de hacer comedias en este tempo* (Bordeaux, 1901).

20. More about the Polish Comic Theatre can be found in the
Anthology of Old Polish Drama, by Julian Lewański, 5 vols.
(Warszawa: Polski Instytut Wydawniczy, 1959).

SELECTED BIBLIOGRAPHY

Besides the bibliographical notes of the preceding Introduction consult, if possible, the following works:

On Comparative Literature and on Bibliography:

Baldensperger, Fernand and Werner F. Friederich, *Bibliography of Comparative Literature.* Chapel Hill: U. of North Carolina Press. 1950.
(Includes the annual supplements of the *Yearbook of Comparative and General Literature.*)
Block, Haskell M. "The Concept of Influence in Comparative Literature," *YCGL* 7. 1958.
Meserole, Harrison T., et al., comps. *1968 MLA International Bibliography.* New York: MLA. 1969.
Weisstein, Ulrich. *Comparative Literature and Literary Theory. Survey and Introduction.* William Riggan, trans. Bloomington: Indiana UP. 1968.
Wellek, René and Austin Warren. *Theory of Literature.* New York: Harcourt Brace. 1942, rpt. 1956.

On authors mentioned in the preceding Introduction:

About the Art of Comedy:

Adams, Hazard, ed. *Critical Theory since Plato.* New York: Harcourt Brace, 1971.
(This anthology presents the major theoretical statements from Plato to the present, arranged chronologically, in an objective manner.)

Altenhofer, N. ed. *Komödie und Gesellschaft, Komödientheorie des neunzehnten Jahrhunderts.* Frankfurt: Athenäum, 1973. (Mostly in German, one essay in French, by K. Hildebrand, "Des Conditions de la bonne comédie.")

About Kleist's comic play *The Broken Jar:*

Delbruck, H. *Kleists Weg zur Komödie.* Untersuchungen zur Stellung des 'Zerbrochenen Jrugs' in einer Typologie des Lustspiels. Studien zur deutschen Literature, 38. Tübingen: Niemayer, 1973.

About Lessing's *Minna von Barnhelm oder Das Soldatenglück:*

Rempel, H. *Tragödie und Komödie im dramatischen Schaffen Lessings.* Bln. 1935.

Metzger, M. M. *Lessing and the Language of Comedy.* Den Haag, 1966. (Diss. Ithaca/N.Y. 1965.)

About Molière's comedies:

Hubert, J. D. *Molière and the Comedy of Intellect.* Berkeley/Los Angeles, 1962.

Lancaster, H. C. "Les Fourberies de Scapin." *French Dramatic Literature in the Seventeenth Century.* H. C. L. Tl. 4/2. Baltimore: 1940. 730-733.

Moore, W. G. "Molière: The Comic Paradox." *Modern Language Review* 68: 771-5. 1973.

About the Comedy in France before Molière:

Guichemerle, R. *La Comédie avant Molière. 1640-1660.* Paris: Armand Colin. 1971.

About Marivaux:

Deloffre, Frédéric. *Marivaux et le marivaudage, une préciosité nouvelle. Etude de langue et de style.* Paris: Société d'Editions Les Belles Lettres. 1955.

McKee, Kenneth. *The Theatre of Marivaux.* New York: NY University Press, 1958.

Tilley, A. "Marivaux" in his Three French Dramatists: Racine, Marivaux, Musset. Cambridge: 1933. Pp. 78-136.

About Musset:

Gochberg, H. S. *Stage of Dreams. The Dramatic Art of A. de Musset. 1828-1834.* Geneva: Droz, 1967. Pp. 97-125.

Sices, David. *Theater of Solitude: The Drama of Alfred de Musset.* Hanover: Nitt, University Press of New England, 1973.

Touge, Frederick. *L'Art du dialogue dans les comédies en prose d'Alfred de Musset. Etude de stylistique dramatique.* Paris: Nizet, 1967.

Van Tieghem, Philippe. "L'Evolution du théâtre de Musset dès le début à Lorenzaccio." *Revue de l'Histoire du Théâtre,* 1957.

About Beaumarchais:

Fredrick, Edna C. *The Plot and Its Construction in Eighteenth Century Cristicism of French Comedy. A Study of Theory with Relation to the Practice of Beaumarchais.* Diss. Bryn Mawr, Pennsylvania, 1934.

Ratermanis, J. B. *The Comic Style of Beaumarchais.* Seattle: Univ. of Washington Press, 1961.

Van Tieghem, Philippe. *Beaumarchais par lui-même.* Paris: Editions du Seuil, 1960.

Critical Studies in Relation to the Practice of Comedy writing in France:

Abirached, R. "Molière et la *commedia dell'arte:* le dénouement du jeu." *Revue d'Histoire du Théâtre* 26: 223-8, 1973.

Lenient, Charles-F. *La Comédie en France au XIXe siècle.* In 2 vols. 1898. II, pp. 303-335. In his *La Comédie.*

Mamczarz, I. "Les Intermèdes comiques italiens au XVIIIe siècle." *Centre National de Recherche Scientifique,* 1972.

Spaziani, M. "La *Commedia dell'Arte* in Francia." *Cultura Scuola,* 32. 1969, 34-47.

About Russian Comedy: Chekhov:

K. S. Stanislavskij. *My Life in Art,* Boston, 1924.

Styan, J. L. *Chekhov in Performance. A Commentary on the Major Plays.* London, 1971.

Valency, M. *The Breaking String: The Plays of A. Tchekhov* Oxford, 1966.

About Gogol:

Lavrin, J. *Nikolaj V. Gogol'.* Norfolk, Conn., 1944.

About Turgenev:

M. Redgrave's "Introduction" to Ivan Sergeevich Turgenev's comedy *A Month in the Country.* London: Hemenionn, 1953.

and numerous Russian publications, to be followed in *YWMLS, PMLA* Bibliographies, and so on.

For more detailed studies of comedy in other countries look also into the index of authors and of works in these bibliographies. A short mini-history of comedy in the European countries cannot include all the countries. There are still Ukrainian, Dutch, Serbo-Croatian, Danish, and other comedies interesting for a survey. An introductory survey of comedies may only indicate the trends of how comedy developed in different European countries. A good way to deepen the knowledge of comedies in other countries and in those mentioned in the Introduction is to do research, taking into consideration the mentioned bibliographical listings, especially in *PMLA* and in *Year's Works in Modern Language Studies,* up to date.

Part I

PHILIPPE QUINAULT
AND HIS COMEDY
THE INDISCREET LOVER,
OR THE MASTER BLUNDERER

INTRODUCTORY NOTE

Philippe Quinault, born in Paris in 1635, was a playwright who wrote comedies, operas, and other plays, mostly in Paris, where he died in 1688. His first works introduced the so-called French *langue précieuse,* a kind of sophisticated language mostly spoken by women of the Parisian high society. This language was appreciated by some poets who tried to give the French language its dignity and purity. Others ridiculed it and its representatives. Among the first was Madame de Sévigné, *une précieuse,* and among the critics and poets who wrote mockeries about the language and the persons who used it, was mainly Molière.

Nicolas Boileau-Despréaux, who codified the rules of dramatic art in his *Art poétique* in 1674, attacked the *préciosité* of Quinault's first plays. Quinault's operas were more appreciated during his lifetime. Today his works are in the shadow. If they are mentioned, however, it is more because of Boileau's sarcasms than in an appreciative manner.

Quinault's *L'Amant Indiscret,* in English *The Indiscreet Lover, or The Master Blunderer** is a comedy in five acts, in

---

*See my translation following this introductory note. The full French title reads: *L'Amant Indiscret ou Le Maistre Estourdi,* according to the spelling of the rare edition of MDCLVII (1657) printed in Paris.

41

verse. Its first performance was at the Hotel de Bourgogne in 1654. Printed in 1664 at Rouen, it was mentioned as having had a printed edition already in 1656 by Toussaint Quinet, as noted in the Dryden Edition of *Sir Martin Mar-All,* under *Source,* but I found the rare edition of 1657 only and used it for my translation.

The Indiscreet Lover by Quinault and Molière's *Blunderer, or The Counterplots* are supposed to have been adaptations of Barbieri's *L'Inavvertito,* composed in 1629. The Italian comedy in prose, in five acts, was produced at Lyons in 1653, then at Béziers for the Prince de Conti and his guests. In Paris it was seen on stage at the Théâtre du Petit-Bourbon on November 3, 1658. There is still a great controversy as to who served as source of inspiration, Molière to Quinault or Quinault to Molière, or whether they both used Barbieri's comedy as a model for their independent adaptation of the *Inavvertito.* The following translation of Quinault's *Indiscreet Lover* and the subsequent analysis may help the student in solving this problem at least partly.

Characters of Quinault's
*The Indiscreet Lover, or The Master Blunderer**

Cleander, Lucresse's lover
Philipin, Cleander's servant
Carpalin, Innkeeper of The Black Head†
Courcaillet, Innkeeper of The Royal Sword‡
Lisipe, another of Lucresse's lovers
Lucresse, Cleander's and Lisipe's mistress
Rosette, Lucresse's maid
Lidame, Lucresse's mother

The play takes place in Paris.

---

*The title "Indiscreet" is not used in the ordinary meaning of this word; it indicates rather an absentminded lover who is a petulant simpleton, in contrast to his servant. Molière's "Etourdi" indicates the same character, who thoughtlessly commits deeds that mar all the plots of his servant.

†Black Head is the translation of the French *Tête Noire,* the actual name of an inn in Paris.

‡The Royal Sword is in French l'*Epée royale.*

ACT I

SCENE 1

CLEANDER, PHILIPIN

CLEANDER: Tell me, is my hope well founded? Did you see their ship?

PHILIPIN: The boat has landed.* A plank was put on board, to stop it. As soon as I arrived, people left it.

CLEANDER: But, did you notice this dear beauty?

PHILIPIN: I saw quite well Lucresse with her mother.

CLEANDER: Are you telling the truth or flattering me? It would be an act of grace if you told me whether you actually saw her.

PHILIPIN: I saw her as well as I see you now.

CLEANDER: It's possible that you only thought you see her.

PHILIPIN: Oh, I'm no dupe. I noticed clearly the color of her skirt, her gait, and I recognized her mother, by hearing her spitting. Besides, I noticed in the crowd a certain blusterer who was leading your mistress.

CLEANDER: It's perhaps a relative of hers.

PHILIPIN: Or a bashful lover. Soon enough this will be clarified.

CLEANDER: Thus I'm going to wait for them in this inn, as you told me.

PHILIPIN: Hurry! According to the letter you received, you may figure out that they will arrive in order to put up at this inn. I'm going to entertain Rosette, their maid, who, as you know, isn't unkind. In the meantime, prepare the innkeeper, and give him your orders. And, above everything else, take care not to commit any blunder.

CLEANDER: I certainly will not fail to do so. Go now. Here's the innkeeper.

---

*Philipin uses here the term *la Coche*. This name was given to a ship used in public service on rivers. (Notes translated from Fournel's French notes.)

SCENE 2

CARPALIN, COURCAILLET, CLEANDER

CARPALIN: In order to get the best drink, sir, please enter my
inn. We don't sell heavy wines from Orléans, we have some
Chablis, some Arbois and some Beaune, besides some Coin-
drieux from the Rhône River vines.

COURCAILLET: Sir, the most delicate wine is found here, it's from
Malaguet, Contepordrix, Muscat, Lasciotat, and from Mal-
voisie. This wine is sweeter than nectar of the gods, sweeter
even than ambrosia.

CARPALIN: Yes, he has these beverages as I have some in my eye.
It's only wine from Nanterre or from Argenteuil. Oh, you would
be well treated in the inn of this shabby poor cat. He has good
wine for those who swoon, it's vinegar.

COURCAILLET: Better than yours.

CARPALIN: You are only a bad cook who works too cheap.

COURCAILLET: Oh, the coarse foul fricassee cook!

CARPALIN: Oh, the impertinent fellow, it's a groom who makes
the currycomb dance.*

COURCAILLET: Sir, enter my place, it's there where the fatted dolt
is skinned.

CARPALIN: Out! Or, if not, your mug will get a drubbing!

CLEANDER: Gentlemen, peace!

CARPALIN: Out, or I'll rub you down!

COURCAILLET: It would cost you very much.

CLEANDER: Pulling my doublet in this manner you tore it in three
places.

CARPALIN: If I took a stick—!

COURCAILLET: That's what I would like to see.

CLEANDER: Don't fight here. This uproar and noise lead the passer-
by astray. Go away. I'm entering here.

---

*Or "makes a market penny."

SCENE 3

CARPALIN, CLEANDER

CARPALIN: Whoever has common sense will certainly come to Black Head, for a drink.

CLEANDER: I did not stop here for drinking wine, but for eating.

CARPALIN: We have some food too. We furnish the most delicious meals, well-prepared souls, on nicely served tables. Our soups are well done and seasoned.

CLEANDER: Some will be necessary.

CARPALIN: Besides, we furnish the best simmered young stuffed pigeons, poultry with mushrooms, titbits of small pork sausage, cardoons chestnuts, kernels of fir cone, fine beef tongue decorated with lemon slices, pomegranate, and egg yolk.

CLEANDER: That's enough.

CARPALIN: We are skillful in preparation of rice with veal, we do it à la princesse, crayfish soups, chicken, game, and fish, or pigeon quail, and young quail.

CLEANDER: We'll need only one, but a really good one.

CARPALIN: If you want four pieces, it's only a question of price, and you'll be well served. Never has paid money seen better soups. I have strong arms, and my hands aren't dead.

CLEANDER: You'll serve an entrée.

CARPALIN: Here, that means hash, beef tongue, white pudding, chicken hash with white sauce, some lamb leg, ham slices, a ragout on a bread crust.

CLEANDER: That's too much.

CARPALIN: It's not too much for whetting the appetite. With regard to roasts, we have fat capons and fat pullets of two pheasants, turtledoves, partridges, bustards, threshers, ducks, lapwings, tealducks, wood pigeons, young woodcocks, curlews, young wild ducks, and plovers.

CLEANDER: Finish that, Master, please.

CARPALIN: We're never short of anything in this inn. If you need sweet side dishes, a capon hash with Corinthian raisins, lamb juice, sprinkled with a bowl of ortolan, jelly, pistachio nuts in a ragout, with almonds rissole.*

CLEANDER: We don't need so much.

CARPALIN: Some fruit from Touraine.

CLEANDER: That's it. This long chitchat kills me. I don't want anything superfluous at the reception.

CARPALIN: If you'd like to have a day of fish party, we can put up with many ways of preparation: for the first dish some healthy soup, crayfish, green peas, smelt, turnips, onion, skate fish, rice, bread soup, salmon, pike, turbot, shad, trout, either fried or served as a casserole, pickled, or chilled.

CLEANDER: Some other day.

CARPALIN: We may put in some baked cake, eggs of several kinds, mushrooms with cream, milt in a ragout.

CLEANDER: Oh, his speech is extremely long.

CARPALIN: A ramekin dish of cheese and artichokes fricassee, jelly and dressing of victuals boiled to keep their white color.

CLEANDER: Enough, enough. Let's talk about the present.

CARPALIN: Sir, it's all aimed to tell you that among all the taverns mine isn't the worst.

CLEANDER: A modest team is supposed to arrive here, and not too much should be served to these people. You'll be well paid. In return you have to keep silent, eh?

CARPALIN: About what? Tell me, please.

CLEANDER: About a love secret.

CARPALIN: About a love secret? That's an outrageous affront I receive. Ah, sir, my forehead is blushing when I hear these words.

CLEANDER: Here are ten golden coins† and that will do. Believe me, if I find happiness in your inn, I'll know how to give honor where honor is due.

CARPALIN: That's exactly what I want. I hate being blamed. You may come here with a lady.

---

*In the seventeenth century, this was a minced meat fritter.

†In the original, "pistoles"—seventeenth-century golden coins having the value of ten francs.

CLEANDER: Yes.

CARPALIN: It's all right. I've learned from scholars one has to live with the living. I don't care about other people's affairs.

CLEANDER: Listen, there will come a girl with her mother and some servants.

CARPALIN: Oh, I understand you well. In good French that means they are good for nothing.

CLEANDER: That's absolutely wrong. Your words irritate. I talk about honorable people of merit.

CARPALIN: People who deserve the honor of receiving the lily flower.*

CLEANDER: Insolent man, use a better language.

CARPALIN: If it's not worse.

CLEANDER: Don't pretend you're afraid. This is ridiculous.

CARPALIN: My house, up to the present, has been immaculate. When I entered it for the first time, I had it painted. Now, I intend to remain in it forever. I don't care about getting rich. Only highly educated people can allow themselves to sin, without being involved in a scandal.

CLEANDER: All right, there's nothing in my plan that could be considered dirty. It's an honest love that rules my desires.

CARPALIN: Living an honorable life would make me happy.

CLEANDER: Is the pot heated?

CARPALIN: No, but it should be placed in the oven.

CLEANDER: It's time to do it. Do you have a fat, well-done capon?

CARPALIN: I'll get some from du Mans; they will be tasty. If they aren't of one delicate and soft piece I'll take them even in little morsels.

CLEANDER: So, you haven't any, for now?

CARPALIN: No.

CLEANDER: Oh, I found here an unpleasant host. Do you have at least chicken for a fricassee?

---

*The lily flower was an ornament characteristic of the ancient armorial bearings of French kings, an emblem of French kingdom. Carpalin uses the words "lily flower" in an ironic manner, since French prisoners condemned to the galleys were branded with the lily flower.

CARPALIN: The gate to Paris isn't too far. I'll take care of it right away.

CLEANDER: Don't you have now anything here? Neither beef nor lamb?

CARPALIN: I expect it from Poissy.

CLEANDER: Anything cooked or ready for cooking?

CARPALIN: I have a little pigeon that may satisfy you.

CLEANDER: That's not enough.

CARPALIN: This bird drowned yesterday when it tried to drink water in our pail. The poor bird died desperately. Nevertheless, my wife has eaten it.

CLEANDER: Do you have some pastry? Or do I stick in the mire?

CARPALIN: Sir, with regard to pastry, our oven is damaged, but I expect a mason to repair it.

CLEANDER: Do people have a good living here?

CARPALIN: Only at this moment, sir. You came inadvertently. You may have a Robert sauce. We have some fresh pork, thin, soft and tender chops.

CLEANDER: That's not enough. Where did they send me to?

CARPALIN: Give me some money, if you're in a hurry, and I will go to get some capon from the cook-shopkeeper.

CLEANDER: Do it, urgently. Have a couple of chickens added. Send for it. Do you have some servants?

CARPALIN: Can you find servants without bad qualities? No, but I have my Barbet, who knows how to turn the iron-pin with meat. He'll be on the way, right now, and he'll be back pretty soon.

CLEANDER: Go. I'll wait for you. Run, please, and don't remain there. My mistress will not have a good living, here, but I shall make it good by looking into her beautiful eyes. Their azure color is clearer than the sky-blue color. Who is the man I see coming here? His presence annoys me. He will be an obstacle to my good fortune.

SCENE 4

CLEANDER, LISIPE

CLEANDER: Is it you, dear Lisipe? Am I not mistaken in seeing you? Am I not abused?

LISIPE: No, dear Cleander, it's me.

CLEANDER: What a happy meeting in this town!

LISIPE: I have worked for a rather long time, having an invisible job where I didn't gain anything but some beating. It's time for me to look for a sweeter chance, on my own. I feel quite worn out, after having performed my military profession. Now, I am looking for a sweet rest; I'm ready to marry a rare beauty. The fulfillment of my wishes would mean for me the utmost of my happiness. I traveled with this beauty from Paris. She came here since a legal action demands her presence here.

CLEANDER: You were supposed to leave our city for three years. I missed news from you.

LISIPE: It is so really, Cleander, but hands that are used for military service have lost the habit of writing often. It's becoming difficult to use them again for writing.

CLEANDER: Then, the remembrance of good friends is lost.

LISIPE: Not at all. I have always remembered Cleander.

CLEANDER: That means I am greatly obliged to you for making me believe it.

LISIPE: Well, I was told that you keep gambling. How are your chances?

CLEANDER: They are decreasing. My Parisian house was sold a month ago. It melted in my hands into pretty coins.

LISIPE: When misfortune keeps striking, people are in distress.

CLEANDER: Whenever I play at dice I bet my own money, and when I forget myself and say *tope** or *masse*† my misfortune

---

*Tope means "Your hand upon it!"

†*Masse* means stakes at play.

does not leave me. If I play a picket card game with an Ostrogoth he will make twenty times a *pique** and then a *repique* and let me be totally defeated, having lost all my tricks. Twenty times against once I used to lose.

LISIPE: Oh, it's no fun to lose in a game!

CLEANDER: I don't want to gamble any longer, and I have sworn not to do it, at least for six weeks.

LISIPE: A gambler's oath is a vain promise. I'm sure you will not keep it.

CLEANDER: I intend to manage the remainder of my property; thus I'm not going to take another harmful chance.

LISIPE: Such self-control seems quite impossible. You are too emotional, with regard to gambling.

CLEANDER: I'm emotional because of another passion.

LISIPE: Do you think of nothing but glory or nothing but love?

CLEANDER: It's love, Lisipe.

LISIPE: In this game, like any other, you are taken in. Often an eager lover is drawn in and becomes a loser playing with his misfortune. Is it a widow or a girl?

CLEANDER: It's the only daughter, the only child of a good family, a wealthy, most beautiful young lady.

LISIPE: Who accepts your courting, doesn't she?

CLEANDER: She doesn't hate me at all.

SCENE 5

LISIPE, PHILIPIN, CLEANDER

LISIPE: Is she a Parisian girl?

PHILIPIN (*aside*): Ha!

CLEANDER: No, she is from Auxerre.

Pique and repique: In the game of a piquet, pique is the scoring of thirty points by the elder hand, before the opponent scores one; a *repique* occurs when the player, instead of reckoning thirty, reckons ninety and counts above ninety as many points as he would above thirty.

PHILIPIN (*aside*): It's his rival.

LISIPE: There I am the owner of some real estate. Would you inform me how this love was taking shape?

CLEANDER: One day, I was in Auxerre in a church.

PHILIPIN (*to* CLEANDER): Sir, what do you think about using this in such a way?

CLEANDER: It's one of my friends.

PHILIPIN: That's not important.

CLEANDER: That's not important? When I see the object of my love appearing so charming, so beautiful, I have to adore it, up to my tomb.

LISIPE: Her name?

PHILIPIN: Be careful!

CLEANDER: Her name is Lucresse.

PHILIPIN: Eh, sir!

LISIPE (*aside*): That's the name of my mistress as well!

CLEANDER: One of her gloves fell, I picked it up for her, and handed it in to her, with a compliment.

PHILIPIN: He's going to tell him everything.

CLEANDER: At this first approach our hearts were thrilled, our souls were softly carried away into our eyes, and learned the emotion of first love. I followed her at a distance of twenty feet, but I was afraid of her mother.

PHILIPIN: Stop!

CLEANDER: Go, you seem too severe! She implored me not to continue following her. Nevertheless, I got her address, and, since that day, I have visited Auxerre several times. I always received there the testimony of her good will.

PHILIPIN: What will he say more?

CLEANDER: My servant knows her maid.

PHILIPIN: The devil may have his part in this.

CLEANDER: This smart young lady was eager to show me trust and love. She promised me she'd never marry anyone else but me.

PHILIPIN: Well, a good start, a nice discovery.

LISIPE: Friend, that was certainly a nice adventure, but why did you come here?

CLEANDER: My mistress will be here soon too, since her mother brings her to this place from Auxerre.

PHILIPIN: What do you say?

CLEANDER: Shut up!

PHILIPIN: Your quartan ague.

CLEANDER: They will stay here, at this inn. The innkeeper is smart. I know how to treat him, in his . . .

PHILIPIN: You talk badly.

CLEANDER: Scoundrel, will you shut up? I'll see this dear beauty at ease.

PHILIPIN: I get mad.

LISIPE: You'll have to be careful regarding her mother.

CLEANDER: In talking to Lidame one could spoil everything.

PHILIPIN: Now, everything is lost.

LISIPE: So, her mother is Lidame?

CLEANDER: Thus you know her?

LISIPE: Yes, I know her as a woman who accepts good advice, knows how to use it, and who would be difficult to be abused. As far as I know, nobody who isn't a descendant from a noble and rich family would get her daughter in marriage. I assure you, in spite of all your endeavor, this mother will never have another son-in-law but myself.

PHILIPIN: Sir, you get it?

LISIPE: Besides, I tell you, she hates gamblers like a plague. Shortly, you will understand it better.

CLEANDER: Lisipe, one more word.

LISIPE: Good-bye, I'll see you.

SCENE 6

PHILIPIN, CLEANDER

PHILIPIN: How funny, what an imprudence to make an actual confidential report to a rival.

CLEANDER: What do you say, Philipin, Lisipe is my rival?

PHILIPIN: Rosette told me so.

CLEANDER: Oh, what an infortunate man I am!

PHILIPIN: According to me it's an incomparable foolishness. Lisipe left Lucresse and her mother in a church. In the meantime, he came here to look for an inn and to make a room reservation. If you hadn't met him and if you were not such a blunderer you would have lived here with your mistress. But you were so eager to tell your amorous adventure! When I was pulling you out you kept on revealing everything about yourself. You have satisfied your talkative mood. From now on, you may turn elsewhere; my plans have been destroyed. You may make some better ones. Such a lack of discretion can't be found anywhere else.

CLEANDER: Oh, don't insult a miserable lover! My despair following my lack of discretion will be enough to punish me. Believe me, my death will soon make an end to my miserable life.

PHILIPIN: Ha! Take care not to do anything of this kind! Let's go in! To serve you yet I'll try to do my best. A remedy for anything may be found, except for death.

Act II

Scene 1

LISIPE, LUCRESSE, ROSETTE

LISIPE: Pretty dear Lucresse, that's the apartment your mother leaves you, according to my wishes.

LUCRESSE: We have to live here, but why did you put us up in this house? This room is small and not elegant. I would feel much better in the other inn.

LISIPE: You would feel better there, but I would feel worse. You would see your lover there, while I would see my rival.

LUCRESSE: What lover? Oh, Lisipe, please be more explicit!

LISIPE: I am explicit enough. I know what's going on. Didn't an obliging wooer date you there?

LUCRESSE: Are you crazy?

LISIPE: No, but jealous. You don't love me very much.

LUCRESSE: That could be.

LISIPE: You know Cleander.

LUCRESSE: So what if I know him? Does such a slight suspicion startle you? Is it a great crime to know him?

LISIPE: It's a crime to love Cleander.

LUCRESSE (*aside*): He knows everything. Too bad!

LISIPE: You are blushing, Lucresse.

LUCRESSE: If I'm blushing, it's because of your weakness, your unjustified suspicions.

LISIPE: Don't flare up, answer my question. Can you deny that you love Cleander, that he was supposed to wait for you in the other inn? Cleander told me all today, without any restraint.

LUCRESSE: Cleander?

LISIPE: Yes, Cleander. I know everything from him. He doesn't care to talk about your feelings for him; he even boasts about it everywhere. Shame on you.

LUCRESSE: Oh, God, what do you say?

LISIPE: I am telling the truth.

LUCRESSE: What a perfidy, what a base action!

LISIPE: Therefore, it is reasonable to disclose everything. In order to punish this ungrateful man, refute all and pay for contempt with hatred and with love for love, this very day. Change a criminal fervor into fire. Lisipe is at least as good as a false lover. Your mother is waiting for me! Good-bye! Think well about what I said. I am a gentleman and will not tell your mother anything. I go with regret, but I have to bring your mother to her attorney.

SCENE 2

LUCRESSE, ROSETTE

LUCRESSE: Apparently, I made a false judgment. Sometimes a well-dressed man may have some bad qualities! Oh, how much this contempt displeases me! How unhappy I am! What a mean-spirited man, this Cleander!

ROSETTE: But . .

LUCRESSE: Don't say a word in favor of this ungrateful lover, and don't set yourself against my resentment. I'm still very weak with regard to this traitor. But what does his servant want, a servant of a perfidious master?

SCENE 3

PHILIPIN, LUCRESSE, ROSETTE

PHILIPIN: Rosette, God bless you.

ROSETTE: Where are you going, unfortunate? If Lidame or Lisipe . . .

PHILIPIN: They both went out.

ROSETTE: They went to our attorney, for some suit. He lives not far from here; they will be back pretty soon.

PHILIPIN: I too will not delay my taking off.

LUCRESSE: What does Philipin tell you, what is he looking for?

PHILIPIN: I'm looking for you, sent by Cleander. Listen.

LUCRESSE: I don't want to hear anything from him.

PHILIPIN: Haughtiness becomes you well, but may I be so proud to have you listen to me, would you?

LUCRESSE: No, go away.

PHILIPIN: Where does this contemptuous humor of hers come from? I never saw her in such a sad mood and so grumbling!

ROSETTE: She has a good reason, for your master . . .

PHILIPIN: What did he do?

ROSETTE: Your master is only an insolent perfectionist, but he does not know how to protect the honor of a lady-lover. Lisipe has heard Lucresse's secrets from him.

LUCRESSE: My kindness made him frivolous and fearless, it's too much for me.

PHILIPIN: Actually, my master is rather thoughtless, and it's due to his frankness only, not maliciousness, that he always commits some act of thoughtlessness. Lisipe is his friend, and I'm quite positive that Cleander wouldn't tell Lisipe anything that might irritate you.

LUCRESSE: Actually, what he said isn't to my benefit.

PHILIPIN: Lisipe is his rival, thus he shouldn't be believed.

LUCRESSE: Whatever he said is confirmed by all you say. Since he showed himself ungrateful, he lost my love.

PHILIPIN: Really, if you knew how my master regrets already all he said, how desperate he is, how he curses himself in a rage, he would even postpone his own death to be able to destroy Lisipe. If you were as furious as a tigress you would feel compassion. You would pity him.

LUCRESSE: I shouldn't. Go and tell him it's hopeless to try to see me again. My love was weaker than my anger now.

PHILIPIN: This would mean the end for my master, his life would be finished.

LUCRESSE: I don't care

PHILIPIN: Damn! What a cruelty!

LUCRESSE: Go without reasoning and tell him I'll never forgive him.

PHILIPIN: Thus you want him to die?

LUCRESSE: After such an outrage, he may die; he will no longer be able to oblige me. Go, go to warn him! Then go! No, return!

PHILIPIN: Finally, what am I supposed to tell him?

LUCRESSE: Tell him . . . No, don't tell him anything.

PHILIPIN: That's a way to tell me there's nothing to be said.

LUCRESSE: My heart is unable to face my justified anger. Though he's a scoundrel I'm unable to hate him. I cannot revenge myself, although he acted as a traitor. . . . If he were still fond of me I would forgive him

PHILIPIN: Ma'am, he adores you. If he does not have the privilege of seeing you tonight he will die a silly death of boredom.

LUCRESSE: How could I see him?

PHILIPIN: Oh, that's easy. If you only would stand by and see him you may choose a date.

ROSETTE: Someone is knocking at the door. What shall we do, for God's sake? It's your boorish lover! I am shaking for fear.

LUCRESSE: I myself shall open the door. Have Philipin enter this closet.

Scene 4

LISIPE, LUCRESSE, PHILIPIN, ROSETTE

LUCRESSE: Oh, you are back so soon?

LISIPE: It's not without a good reason.

LUCRESSE: What reason?

LISIPE: The attorney is not at home.

LUCRESSE: Did my mother remain there to wait for him?

LISIPE: No, she went into her room. In the meantime, I'm going to look for some papers that are necessary to be shown first, at the trial.

LUCRESSE: Where do you want to go?

LISIPE: I'm going to take our suitcase into this closet where our innkeeper has put it.

LUCRESSE: Remain here, for God's sake.

PHILIPIN: If he sees me, I'm dead.

LISIPE: In keeping me here you seem very confused. Why?

PHILIPIN: That's it, upon my word!

LUCRESSE: I'm going to explain it to you. Listen, I have much to tell you. I want to reveal an important conspiracy against you. Philipin is here.

PHILIPIN: Here I'm caught, I, the silly one.

LISIPE: What Philipin?

LUCRESSE: Cleander's servant.

PHILIPIN: Now for sure, I'll be the villain. He'll be told about everything.

LUCRESSE: Philipin came here to ask me to agree to a date.

PHILIPIN: Where shall I hide myself?

LUCRESSE: I'm still speechless about his words.

PHILIPIN: To come out cheap I can expect at least my arm to be put out of joint.

LISIPE: Oh, if I got him here, this damned Philipin!

PHILIPIN: I was never so close to death!

LISIPE: What did you answer, dear and beautiful Lucresse?

LUCRESSE: I've cheated this servant.

PHILIPIN: Oh, the traitress!

LUCRESSE: To whatever he said I pretended agreeing, with the goal in mind to warn you and to complain about your distrust.

PHILIPIN: Oh, poor Philipin, it's time to think about your conscience!

LISIPE: Cleander's plan is to kidnap you. Ma'am, where are you supposed to meet him?

LUCRESSE: On the Royal Square.

PHILIPIN: She puts on the wrong scent!

LISIPE: Oh, this vile rival! I have to think about a revenge!

LUCRESSE: Where are you running, Lisipe?

LISIPE: Don't stop me, I'm going to your date to find him on the spot.

SCENE 5

LUCRESSE, ROSETTE, PHILIPIN

LUCRESSE: Have Philipin come in.

ROSETTE: Hurry up! Come out right now

PHILIPIN: You've tried my patience enough. Even if I had fever I wouldn't have shaken so much. But now, I have to leave to see my master. Will he not see you sometimes, at least at the door?

LUCRESSE: Yes, tell him he may talk to me for a little while, as soon as he sees my mother and my lover leave this place.

PHILIPIN: Regarding your lover, I expect he will no longer importune you and your mother.

LUCRESSE: Are you sure?

PHILIPIN: I'm positive. For this purpose our innkeeper is already prepared. He is supposed to disguise himself, but this is a secret I wanted to keep from the sight of my master blunderer. I'm not anxious to have him torment us by spoiling everything in the belief that he's doing the right thing. But this secret will not be kept from you.

ROSETTE: Oh, God, the door is open and here is your jealous lover!

Scene 6

LISIPE, LUCRESSE, PHILIPIN, ROSETTE

LISIPE: You didn't indicate the time of your date! But what does this rascal want here?

PHILIPIN: I want to tell you something of great importance.

LISIPE: Talk.

PHILIPIN: It's only face to face that I would tell you a secret.

ROSETTE: I'll consider him very smart if he stands out.

PHILIPIN *(to* LISIPE*)*: Ordered by Cleander, I came here to sound Lucresse's virtue, cunningly. I was able to touch her emotions by my words so well that I got my master a date with her. Now, being aware of your love, far from offending you, my master will refrain from taking advantage of this date, in your favor. He wants you to realize, through this change of mind, that he is a better friend than a discreet lover. He's no longer courting this beauty and wants me to let you know that you may keep watching her.

LISIPE: For such good news take this diamond. I'm most obliged to your master.

PHILIPIN: Good God, what a change!

LISIPE: Ma'am, Philipin, ordered by his master, has just informed me of the truth regarding your date. I wasn't wrong taking Cleander's friendship for granted.

LUCRESSE: *(aside)*: The defeat is good and Lisipe is a dupe.

Scene 7

LISIPE, CARPALIN *disguised as a peasant,*
PHILIPIN, LUCRESSE, ROSETTE

LISIPE: What does this man want from us here?

PHILIPIN: He seems to be an innocent . . . It's our host. Ma'am, please help to play our trick.

CARPALIN: Excuse me, sir, I was told that I'd find here a certain Lisipe!

LISIPE: Yes, that's my name. Do you intend to talk to me?

CARPALIN: I prefer remaining silent. I'm one of your father's farmers. Oh, the poor late man. Sir, thinking of his misfortune I can only cry.

LISIPE: What misfortune? Did my father have some losses?

CARPALIN: The greatest he ever suffered

LISIPE: Which one?

CARPALIN: You'll hear about it soon enough, with expenses.

LISIPE: Tell me everything, it's too much for me to be in suspense.

CARPALIN: My heart tells me not to let you remain in uncertainty. Your Uncle Arbiran gave me a letter for you. There will be news regarding the reason why I'm crying.

LISIPE: Hurry! Give me the letter!

CARPALIN: You'll get it right away, but it's not here.

LISIPE: I'm mortally impatient. Look for the letter in the other pocket, but more carefully

CARPALIN: Yes, sir. I'll find it certainly. I think I've caught it.

LISIPE: Check it right away!

CARPALIN: I don't read well enough if letters are badly written. I have to get my glasses.

LISIPE: That's a waste of time. Give me the paper. *(He reads.)* "To Mr. Paul Grimaud, cobbler-apprentice."

CARPALIN: Oh, it's not for you, it's for my late godfather's cousin's nephew's brother's son.

LISIPE: Hurry, find the other letter addressed to me.

CARPALIN: I'm looking for it.

LISIPE: Do you know what it is all about?

CARPALIN: Yes, sir. Nevertheless, I should find the letter.

LISIPE: That's too great a test for my patience

CARPALIN: Sir, I'm quite positive I must have let it fall down on the boat, when I was pulling out my purse and my handkerchief, when I had to pay the boatman's fare.

LISIPE: Don't keep me in suspense any longer! Tell me right away what I was to be acquainted with

CARPALIN: Shall I say it, sir?

LISIPE: Say it, without further delay!

CARPALIN: Your late father has passed away; that's all you have to know.

LISIPE: My sorrow is deep and my loss is great. But my father was in good health when I left!

CARPALIN: The sickness took him by surprise as soon as you left. Several hours later he was dead. People call this kind of sickness "puncture."*

LISIPE: Or rather pleurisy.

CARPALIN: Yes, sir, that's right. We are not highly educated people and speak a coarse language.

LISIPE: Ma'am, in order to arrange the inheritance after my dad's passing away, it will be necessary for me to make a trip to my place.

LUCRESSE: My mother would do the wrong thing if she stood in your way. When are you leaving?

LISIPE: In an hour or so. I cannot but leave, but I hope to be back, with you, soon.

SCENE 8

CLEANDER, LISIPE, CARPALIN, PHILIPIN, ROSETTE, LUCRESSE

LISIPE: Oh, I see that Cleander is here. Friend, let me hug you!

LUCRESSE (aside): He seems not to like this welcome.

PHILIPIN (aside): No doubt he came only to fight him.

CLEANDER: Lisipe, I think a secret talk with you would be important.

LISIPE: I don't think so; I know the reason why you came. I have been informed; thus I got over our dispute. What do I owe you for such a great effort?

---

*"Puncture," in French crevasion (referring to a bicycle tire), has been used here since it is a slang term for death. The French text uses punaisie, i.e., a nasal ulcer making the breath putrid. "Puncture" is funnier in a comedy.

CLEANDER: What have you been informed about? You surprise me very much.

ROSETTE: He is going to discover everything.

PHILIPIN: That's quite possible.

LISIPE: Philipin has told me everything.

CLEANDER: And what did this traitor tell you?

LISIPE: He told me about your secret plan regarding your date.

PHILIPIN: Sir!

CLEANDER: You will feel how heavy my strokes are.

LISIPE: Why an artifice? What's the good of that if it may be seen through very easily. Since you renounce Lucresse . . .

CLEANDER: What? I'm renouncing?

PHILIPIN: Yes, you told me so.

CLEANDER: Ha! Rascal!

PHILIPIN: Sir, don't be so bewildered.

CLEANDER *(in a whisper)*: I respect this place, rogue! But I swear a hundred strokes will pay you for your swindling.

PHILIPIN *(to LISIPE)*: My master just told me the whole secret. He is generous, but still more discreet. In yielding the way to Lucresse he believes it wouldn't be fair to avow it in her presence. He is more cautious than he seems to be.

LISIPE: He is right and I'm wrong in urging him.

LUCRESSE: I will no longer importune you. I'm leaving to join my mother. *(She talks to CLEANDER)* Pretend, love, hope, and you'll be loved.

LISIPE: Friend, what did she say? I should like to know.

PHILIPIN: I've heard well; I was just nearby. She just reproached him. Say yes.

CLEANDER: Yes, Lisipe.

LISIPE: Oh, I suspected that. I never saw a nobler man than you.

CLEANDER *(looking at CARPALIN)*: Here is Carpalin ridiculously dressed up. Where does this disguise come from?

CARPALIN *(aside)*: Sir, what are you going to say?

LISIPE: Do you know this man?

CLEANDER: Yes, I know him quite well.

LISIPE: He came to tell me bad news about my father's death.

PHILIPIN *(to CARPALIN)*: I told you his brains are weak.

CLEANDER: How come he knew about your father's death before
 you did?

PHILIPIN: That is . . .

CLEANDER: Let me talk. Don't interrupt. This man is from Paris.

LISIPE: That's a great error. It's one of my farmers

CLEANDER: You are mistaken. I should know since I live in his inn.

CARPALIN: I'm going to be paid well for my good will!

LISIPE: What? You cheat! You evildoer! You said that my dad . . .

CARPALIN: Is in good health. Don't become angry.

CLEANDER: If you want a pardon, tell us the whole truth.

LISIPE: Inform us who sent you.

PHILIPIN: Now, everything is marred.

CLEANDER: Talk!

CARPALIN (to CLEANDER): It's for your sake that I was supposed to
 arrange this trick.

PHILIPIN: Imbecile! Drunkard! You have lied.

LISIPE: Kill this rascal!

PHILIPIN: Certainly, I'll not fail to do this.

CARPALIN: What? Philipin, you traitor!

PHILIPIN: Not another word! Go!

SCENE 9

CLEANDER, LISIPE

CLEANDER: Do you think I'd be able to be such a poltroon?

LISIPE: I know too well what I owe you. You have yielded the
 way to Lucresse to me and you made unnecessary my long
 trip I was about to start. I know your noble and pure sincerity.
 No cheating in front of you. I would be insane if I suspected
 you.

SCENE 10

CLEANDER, PHILIPIN, LISIPE, COURCAILLET

PHILIPIN: I have just done the job. He will be crippled for more
 than a week.

COURCAILLET: Sir, someone is waiting for you in the next room. Dinner is served.

LISIPE: I'm going there following you. Friend, come and join us at a poor meal!

CLEANDER: I have just eaten. Go, you keep someone waiting for you. Perhaps some other time, yes.

LISIPE: Good-bye, dear Cleander. I am not ungrateful. Believe me, you may share all my goods as if they were yours.

CLEANDER (*to* PHILIPIN): Is your shrewdness well understood? I cannot often visit my mistress. Lisipe has been made a dupe and I am the sharpest of you all. He believes I'm his friend. What do you say now, Philipin?

PHILIPIN: Me? I say I'm mad, and you, as usual, are ruining everything while you think you are doing well. You are tempted to be indiscreet and reveal our host on this occasion.

CLEANDER: That's how I convinced Lisipe of my sincerity.

PHILIPIN: That's how my master has shown how silly he is. Whatever our host said he did it in your favor. He has disguised himself in order to serve you and thought he would be useful in your love affair. Lisipe was about to leave Lucresse and this town. Before he returned you would have easily made Lucresse agree to be kidnapped.

CLEANDER: Oh, what have I said? What did I do? How miserable I am!

PHILIPIN: On my word, your imprudence is a hopeless sickness.

CLEANDER: Don't accuse me. Accuse my misfortune and don't condemn my complaint and sorrow.

PHILIPIN: This is a lesson that sometimes complaining is a man's lot. But let's talk now about some other trick to be played on Lisipe.

CLEANDER: What trick?

PHILIPIN: We have to figure it out, but let's leave this place where we may be overheard.

CLEANDER: What are you afraid of?

PHILIPIN: I'm afraid of everything in such a situation. The walls, sir, sometimes the walls prick up someone's ears.

Act III

Scene 1

ROSETTE, PHILIPIN

ROSETTE: A thousand curses on cruel men! With his silly talking he has hurt us without striking a blow, this blunderer Cleander, whose lightmindedness seems to enjoy driving us mad.

PHILIPIN: You see how your anger yields to your concern. Let's talk about a remedy, no longer about evil. Regarding generosity, my master is matchless. I don't care whether he's silly or liberal. You can be sure that for your assistance you'll be well rewarded. And, to give you real proof, here are two gold coins.

ROSETTE: Will I get more?

PHILIPIN: Beyond any doubt, Rosette. If my master is happy our fortune is made.

ROSETTE: These golden pieces are bright, but their brightness doesn't affect me. Nevertheless, I accept them to avoid your anger. I myself am very generous, and if I serve Cleander, it is because I have friendly feelings for him. It's too bad to see a loyal lover with the heart of a prince, but the mind of a horse. I pity him.

PHILIPIN: Truce to mockeries. Now, let's talk reasonably about our own plans. We have to eliminate Lisipe from here.

ROSETTE: No man was ever so odious to me; I hate him for his distrust and severe mood. I'm ready to do anything to drive him out of here.

PHILIPIN: Let's act in such a way that we can be sure of success. Do you know where the documents pertaining to the lawsuit are?

ROSETTE: They are locked up in our room, in our suitcase, wrapped in three bags of coarse gray linen; and in another bag of old black velvet is the most important and most precious document. I did the wrapping myself.

PHILIPIN: Well, carefully hide the bag with the important papers. When you are approached about them, cry and, seeming humiliated, say you are afraid you have forgotten them.

ROSETTE: Yes, but what plan do you have?

PHILIPIN: Can't you figure it out? Lisipe will be the first to leave, in order to get them, and we'll get rid of this jealous lover.

ROSETTE: If this is his only concern, go ahead, the cow belongs to us. But, do you know a servant who would be loyal in Lidame's service? He needs one.

PHILIPIN: Oh, this is not good news! Can't you introduce me as this servant-candidate?

ROSETTE: That will be easy! Yes, you'll make it. Here's Cleander. Take care not to tell him anything about our plans; he could ruin them. Your master is a fool.

PHILIPIN: Go home and don't worry.

SCENE 2

CLEANDER, ROSETTE, PHILIPIN

CLEANDER: Rosette, listen, one word only.

ROSETTE: Some other time, please.

PHILIPIN: Sir, she's busy, she has to go to her mistress.

CLEANDER: Stop, it's only for a little while.

ROSETTE: I have no spare time; my mistress waits for me.

CLEANDER: But I wish to tell you something.

ROSETTE: She'll scold me, and you'll be the guilty one for her scolding me. Good-bye.

CLEANDER: This welcome doesn't satisfy me, and my four golden coins don't improve things. Did you give her the four golden coins?

PHILIPIN: Here you are with your question! My conscience has been clean, always!

CLEANDER: All four coins?

PHILIPIN: Yes, all four, what did you think? Your suspicions offend me. You should know me as an honorable man. If you don't believe me, look for another servant, and I'll look for another master!

CLEANDER: My dear Philipin, excuse me, please. Really, I'm wrong in suspecting your loyalty. Please, don't leave me; I know you're innocent. Without you I'd lose all hope.

PHILIPIN: Yes, know I'm worth my weight in gold, and a clever servant is a rare treasure.

CLEANDER: Your luck should be linked with mine. Don't leave me alone the whole day. I feel eager to play a trick, but I'm afraid of its success, and I'm right to be afraid. If you don't oppose the devil tempting me, my purse will lose its weight pretty soon.

PHILIPIN: That should be your primary concern.

CLEANDER: Lucresse is at the door; we have to accost her.

SCENE 3

CLEANDER, PHILIPIN, LUCRESSE

CLEANDER: Adorable marvel, what kind of gracious miracle brings you to me, miserable me? The happy chance of being in your presence takes away all the memory of my past problems. Your bright beauty alleviates the grief of my problems, exciting my joy. As you know, between a couple of lovers silence is more expressive than any reasoning.

LUCRESSE: Alas!

CLEANDER: You sigh, my dear mistress?

LUCRESSE: It's beyond my control if I'm sighing, but you may also explain it as a sign of my weakness, since in my heart love conquers anger, and sighs out of grief for having done so for you. It complains secretly about the inconceivable charm that makes you likable, in spite of your bad qualities, and, through some progression beyond words, when I wish to hate you I must love you.

CLEANDER: I endure all from you: a cruel injury becomes sweet when pronounced by such a beautiful mouth. I wouldn't complain, even if you sentenced me to death. Yes, you are an adorable beauty. You may say that an imprudence like mine doesn't exist. Actually, it's my turn to say that a love like mine cannot be perceived.

LUCRESSE: I believe it, but I tremble with fear that anyone could find us together, by surprise.

CLEANDER: Indeed, if Lisipe meets me in your company we may be afraid of his jealous spirit that makes him capable of doing anything. I was senseless to reveal the trick played on him by my host. It makes me mad when I think that I myself caused this troublesome person to stay here.

LUCRESSE: In this case I am the one to be pitied. He thinks he will inspire me with love for him, while he only scares me. His compliment is but an eternal reproach, for he is rather a boss than a lover. My mother backs him up and he's aware of this fact; thus he treats me like a slave, not like a mistress.

CLEANDER: I'll avenge this indecency. He may be afraid of an irritated lover. His insolence will be followed by his fall. There are only two possibilities: either he will suffer death or I'll lose my life.

LUCRESSE: If I still have some power over your soul you may prove it by dropping such a plan. In using weapons you never know who will be the winner. Your blood would cause me to cry. I become quite uncertain in considering such a problem. My love for you is stronger than my hatred for Lisipe.

PHILIPIN: Lisipe is coming. Ma'am.

LUCRESSE: Heaven, I'm lost!

CLEANDER: I hardly can control my anger, seeing him.

SCENE 4

LISIPE, CLEANDER, LUCRESSE, PHILIPIN

LISIPE: Cleander doesn't keep his promise. That's not the right way to remain friends. He coaxes Lucresse when she's alone with him, and in the street as well. His banished passion has evidently returned now. If he becomes my rival he should be aware of the end of our friendship.

CLEANDER: In losing your friendship I wouldn't lose much.

LISIPE: I guess the reason for such a new scornful attitude. Don't constrain yourself; avow it frankly.

CLEANDER: I constrain myself very little in keeping such a friendship.

LISIPE: Are you very fond of Lucresse?

CLEANDER: Maybe.

PHILIPIN: Is there a sillier kind of speaking still possible? He is kindhearted, but his judgment isn't sound

LISIPE: I see we don't feel well together.

CLEANDER: Yes, you should be afraid of me, more than you imagine.

LISIPE: That's too much!

CLEANDER: That's not enough. You have not yet arrived where you planned.

LISIPE: You fool, you have lost your temper!

LUCRESSE: That's right. Who would sustain such a moody temper? When Cleander declares ingeniously that he is more your friend than my lover? While he speaks in your favor, with concern, when he states on oath that his rest depends upon your happiness and that he'll be glad if you're happy, you are full of pride and you threaten him and you fight, instead of being grateful to Cleander! Such manners surprise him, and he's right when he declares he cannot stand it, without losing his temper.

LISIPE: Is that so? Did you talk to my love about me?

PHILIPIN (aside): Sir, you have to lie.

CLEANDER: That's true.

PHILIPIN: Well, that's a good manner of speaking.

LISIPE: Friend, forgive me! I have been wrong doubting in your loyalty as a friend. Excuse a distrustful attitude of a man in love who is never sure of anything and who takes fright at everything. I am now out of error and I promise you under oath never again to be so suspicious. To give you a proof of it, I leave this beauty under your care. While I'm in a hurry to leave her and this place I entrust you with this precious deposit.

LUCRESSE: What? Did something happen in your home?

LISIPE: No, I am leaving in the service of your mother. I'll go to her to pick up some forgotten papers she needs very badly. Good-bye, loyal friend. See her often and talk to her sometimes about Lisipe's heart he left her. And you, dear beauty, please accept the presence of your lover's friend.

PHILIPIN: That's going all right, this trick has been well played. Now, in order to start the next one, let's find Rosette.

SCENE 5

LUCRESSE, CLEANDER

LUCRESSE: Well, what would you say about this event? Lisipe has been strongly mistaken.

CLEANDER: You were very skillful in putting him on the wrong scent; any other man would become as weak as Lisipe. That's again a success. It makes me appreciate the charming art of your words.

LUCRESSE: Thank God, I'll no longer be followed by an obtrusive man, at any time. Up to his return you could sometimes come and see me. Now, we only have to be afraid of my mother, who is less suspicious than severe.

CLEANDER: This chance is not so great, and the happy moments will pass sooner than we may figure it out. My importunate rival will be back in three days, and he'll destroy my happiness but not my love.

LUCRESSE: Philipin can be of good use to you, delaying Lisipe's return with a trick played on him.

CLEANDER: Delaying Lisipe's return means renewing my joy. Nevertheless, he'll see you again, and sooner or later my hope will come to an end. Lisipe will come and compel you to marry him. That means hastening Cleander's death and the day of your marriage.

LUCRESSE: Let's forget an evil that has not yet arrived. You know my heart's secret. As soon as our legal proceedings are over, the marriage has to take place. But, if I don't change my mother's mind until then, I'll know how to throw myself either into Cleander's arms or into those of Death, in spite of any efforts undertaken by my mother.

SCENE 6

LIDAME, LUCRESSE, CLEANDER
Lidame coming from the inn.

LIDAME: My daughter with a man? What an impudence!

CLEANDER *(about to kiss* LUCRESSE's *hands)*: How can I thank you for this kindness? My heart tries to pass on your hands . . .

LIDAME *(interrupting him)*: . . . in bowing down low, take care not to hurt yourself.

LUCRESSE: It's my mother. What a misfortune!

CLEANDER: My misery is boundless. If I have . . .

LIDAME: Go home, without delay.

CLEANDER: Let me talk to you.

LIDAME: It's not necessary. You're too courteous, too careful.

CLEANDER: But, ma'am, I'm . . .

LIDAME: You'll have too little decency if you see my daughter again. Don't dare to come here again or—you'll not come off so cheap as this time.

CLEANDER: Let's go home. But, I see Philipin walking. I'm going to gamble now, in order to divert my troubles.

SCENE 7

LIDAME, LUCRESSE

LIDAME: Oh, oh, little idiot, you take some liberties. You let him kiss your hands. Was that with your permission?

LUCRESSE: Your suspicion offends me; you wrong me greatly.

LIDAME: Oh, that's too bad. You're a hypocrite. You dare meet me with a flat denial of what I have seen. Tell me the truth;

you'll feel much better. Who's this handsome fellow? I'm confusing you!

LUCRESSE: It's Lisipe's best friend. Lisipe asked him instantly, before leaving, to attend me carefully; he also asked me to agree. You have treated him wrongly. I'm afraid Lisipe would have complaints about it.

LIDAME: Did Lisipe plan to have him take the liberty of kissing your hand?

LUCRESSE: He didn't think about it.

LIDAME: But I saw him bent over your hand.

LUCRESSE: He did so in order to see better the ring Lisipe gave me, and he admired it.

LIDAME: If this is the truth my failure isn't great. People believe in what they see

LUCRESSE: But this friend left irritated.

LIDAME: My daughter, some other time his welcome will be better.

SCENE 8

ROSETTE, LIDAME, LUCRESSE

ROSETTE: Good news, ma'am. A young, prudent, loyal servant has been offered to us. He knows how to cajole and how to recite by heart. In the past, he was an attorney's clerk. In legal matters he can act like a devil. I think his clothes are made from a strong new material. You would not have to spend a penny for his suit of clothes at least for a whole year of service.

LIDAME: That's all right. Have him come right away.

LUCRESSE: What? Is that Philipin?

ROSETTE: Here he comes: (*To* PHILIPIN) You see my mistress. Go and greet her. (*To* LUCRESSE) Ma'am, please, contribute kindly to this trick

LUCRESSE: If this man is a simpleton he doesn't seem so; he will be able to succeed in any plan.

ROSETTE (*to* LIDAME): He is ours, ma'am, straight as dice coins.

LIDAME: I think like you; he doesn't seem awkward.

PHILIPIN: I haven't deserved the merit to have the pleasure to please you. You still don't know all I can do. Appearances often deceive the finest eyes. Sometimes a pretty body covers a shrewd mind. If I have the chance to become one of your attendants, some day, you may find out my skills.

LIDAME: This fellow isn't foolish, as I have figured out.

LUCRESSE: It's not possible to speak better.

ROSETTE: He talks like an angel, upon my word.

LIDAME: I want you to enter my services; it will be a benefit for you, but first we have to agree on your wages.

PHILIPIN: They will be reasonable, I know. I don't doubt we would never be at a variance with you, in this regard. I hope my services will find a fair reward, when you convince yourself that I'm a priceless servant.

ROSETTE: But we need a respondent in lawsuits.

PHILIPIN: Don't worry. I can furnish you with a dozen of them. Shall I go to find one?

LIDAME: I'm not in a hurry. Let's go in . . .

PHILIPIN: My word, am I dreaming or is it a good start?

Scene 9

CLEANDER, PHILIPIN, LIDAME

CLEANDER (*stopping* PHILIPIN): Here you are, scoundrel, fool, of your own free will. You stroll around when I need you! Why didn't you follow me?

LIDAME: What a noise!

CLEANDER: I wouldn't have lost twenty coins of gold.

PHILIPIN: It's not my fault when you lost in gambling.

CLEANDER: If I had found you I would have done something else.

PHILIPIN: Could he spoil our trick better?

CLEANDER: You traitor, I should kill you.

PHILIPIN: Don't be foolish.

CLEANDER (*beating him*): You dare make a trifle of it.

PHILIPIN: What a bore! He hits hard

LIDAME: Why do you strike my servant in such a way?

CLEANDER: He is mine, ma'am.

PHILIPIN: Go to hell, you blunderer! Here's another proof of your foolishness.

CLEANDER: Ma'am, you are mistaken in his identity.

LIDAME: No, that's my servant. Go and beat yours.

CLEANDER: You are wrong yourself. I am quite positive; he has eaten my food for more than a year. Nevertheless, if you need him, in order to please you, I may get rid of him. A moment ago, you treated me badly; now, I shouldn't be less courteous with you, ma'am.

LIDAME: I know you are innocent, and I would apologize. I am confused by this free behavior. Sir, you may dispose of this servant. I refuse to take him, if offered in this manner. I am not always in an offensive mood. Thank you, and good-bye. I'm your humble servant, sir.

SCENE 10

CLEANDER, PHILIPIN

CLEANDER: Everything is going well now. I have succeeded; Lidame is becoming tamed. What do you think?

PHILIPIN: Oh, my shoulder!

CLEANDER: Excuse me, I was angry.

PHILIPIN: Let him go, this rascal, fool, of his own free will. If this is your opinion about me, you're wrong. You have abused me and you have beaten me. I protest. You'll pay for this, and I will make you smart.

CLEANDER: I'll pay you with this last golden coin. Your eyes enjoy it.

PHILIPIN: The strokes I got are worth more than one golden coin.

CLEANDER: I promise you another one in our inn. Don't be the smart one; talk without flattering me.

PHILIPIN: You have beaten me foolishly. Through these strokes you are cast down. I was about to introduce myself into Lidame's service, where I would have had a hundred means to support your love, to take care of her rigorous mind, to supplant Lidame, and to make you happy.

CLEANDER: Oh, my misfortune!

PHILIPIN: Less misfortune than imprudence. Excuse me, I say what I think.

CLEANDER: Oh, my disgrace! Heavens, I'm in despair.

PHILIPIN: The evil is great, but it still may be restored to a sound state. I promise to finish a plan as soon as I shall touch the promised money.

CLEANDER: How?

PHILIPIN: Don't be mistrustful. Give me the money; then everything will be okay.

CLEANDER: Come and get it. Let's go back.

PHILIPIN: That's what I want. Sometimes, the losers don't pay.

ACT IV

SCENE 1

ROSETTE, PHILIPIN, *coming from different sides*

ROSETTE: I have to look for Philipin tonight.

PHILIPIN: I need Rosette; I must see her

ROSETTE: Okay, my trip is done.

PHILIPIN: My running is finished.

ROSETTE: Welcome, Philipin. I'm glad to meet you.

PHILIPIN: Rosette, I'm glad to find you.

ROSETTE: I was going to your lodging.

PHILIPIN: And I was going to yours.

ROSETTE: I have to tell you quite a bit.

PHILIPIN: I'll tell you a lot as well.

ROSETTE: You'll know . . .

PHILIPIN: I'll inform you . . .

ROSETTE: . . . that I believe . . .

PHILIPIN: . . . that it seems to me . .

ROSETTE: We'll not understand each other if we talk simultaneously. Listen to me . .

PHILIPIN: Well, hurry, talk. Women always like to prattle.

ROSETTE: You know I believe that with some skill you will be able to reestablish yourself in the service of my mistress. I've managed her mind, which is not very cunning, and I did it so well that she regrets having refused you. Tell her you have been fired for cursing Cleander. You will soon have her reestablishing you in her service. She just left through this little door, and I wanted to warn you about this fact. She certainly went to her attorney. Be prepared to compliment her and keep your tongue sharpened. Lidame is very easily deceived.

PHILIPIN: That's a good reasoning, but listen, I'm going to give you some advice: It seems I've found the means to bring our lovers to the ultimate climax of joy. This house next to our abode is a lodging furnished with beautiful furniture, and it has vacancies, for the moment. The owner is a relative of my host who hopes to lead Lidame there tonight, through a certain slope.

ROSETTE: Lidame! That's a good joke; how could he do it?

PHILIPIN: As you told me she often regrets her brother, who lost his hunger for our daily bread in a swordfight with an enemy. Being afraid of some powerful relatives, Lidame's brother took to his heels in a hurry. Since then she hasn't heard any news about her brother and has lost hope of ever seeing him again.

ROSETTE: It's true she often grieves and cries in remembrance of this brother, but that doesn't concern us, Philipin.

PHILIPIN: No? do you think so? Haven't you told me he was only sixteen years of age when he left Auxerre and his parents? Thirty years have passed since this misfortune. It's a long time, sufficient to change a man. Lidame is a little silly, and our host will say today that he is her brother, and, he'll pass for him. In a nice coat, received from some secondhand clothes, he'll pretend to lure her into his inn, then into the next building, where my master will be able to dispose of her freely.

ROSETTE: That's a good plan. Here's your host. Doesn't he have the air of a man of importance?

SCENE 2

ROSETTE, PHILIPIN, CARPALIN, *disguised in merchant's clothes*

CARPALIN: Here I am, a brave man like a rabbit.

PHILIPIN: Sir, you smell like an important person, having become "better."

CARPALIN: That's true, Philipin. I've cursed the fat that makes me feel heavy. I cannot find clothes large enough to get into.

ROSETTE: Seeing him so dressed up people could think he is a great monopoly owner or some usurer full of pride.

CARPALIN: By God, this should become true! I'd enjoy a good cheer, but, we have to be reasonable. Let's talk a little about our business. Tell me in detail all you know about the role I'm supposed to be entrusted with. I must know the habits of this absent brother in the past. Tell me everything Lidame could have mentioned.

ROSETTE: If I had to tell you everything in this regard it would take about eight days. She talks about him at practically any occasion.

SCENE 3

LIDAME, CLEANDER, PHILIPIN

LIDAME: I'm very obliged to you for your attendance. I'd like to give you some advice. I'll tell Lisipe, when he returns, about your part in anything regarding his affairs. Good-bye, I'm going to my room. The day is almost over; come and visit me here tomorrow.

CLEANDER: Allow me to show you to your apartment.

LIDAME: No, sir, it's late. Don't worry; I'll get along.

CLEANDER: Well, here's my servant. It's all right, all right. Believe me, I'm a witty man.

PHILIPIN: I don't believe it.

CLEANDER: I've just played a trick everyone should admire.

PHILIPIN: What kind of a trick?

CLEANDER: Listen, I'm going to tell you. When I was walking by myself, I met by chance Lidame. She was coming from her attorney. While shaking hands with her I took the liberty of talking cunningly about you to her.

PHILIPIN: I doubt it.

CLEANDER: Finally, I said that I had fired you, but that you had served me well.

PHILIPIN: That's a good start.

CLEANDER: I said few persons are as cunning as you, you serve in a wonderful manner, and so on, continuing to praise you in the highest superlatives.

PHILIPIN: That means your talk was done with a good all-around intelligence.

CLEANDER: But . . .

PHILIPIN: Bless me with this "but"!

CLEANDER: No, you will be surprised how I turned over a new leaf. In order to avoid suspicions I portrayed you in a strange manner, I did it mingling the blame with praise, in a fair way. I said I knew you as a liar, subtle, sly, malicious, bigoted, false, an impostor who became lazy on purpose, and, for money, you would do anything.

PHILIPIN: You said that.

CLEANDER: That's not all; you'll admire me when I say everything, up to the point. I said she should be careful not to leave you often with her daughter. Possibly any lover could have brought you to give her dangerous advice; thus she should not trust you too much; otherwise, she could be deceived without believing she was.

PHILIPIN: Is that the clever trick of your great wit?

CLEANDER: The good woman believes all I said. She thinks I am sincerity itself and that my friendship for Lisipe is at its highest point. Having thanked me for my good advice, she invited me to visit her often.

PHILIPIN: That means work well done.

CLEANDER: Your judgment cheers me up. You say I've done all right?

PHILIPIN: Yes, looking down the nose, you are a bore; you have just lent a brush to Lidame, laying up a rod for your own back. Your tongue is impertinent; it spoiled the whole plot. Your cursed tittle-tattle is very pernicious. If you had kept quiet you'd be better now.

CLEANDER: Tell me about the plot.

PHILIPIN: Oh! I don't care! I'd be afraid of your foolishness and of your tittle-tattle! You would make some admirable trick of it again. A revealed secret is no longer a secret.

CLEANDER: So, I shouldn't know anything about the plot?

PHILIPIN: No. Please enter here, then go and see whether I am in our inn.

SCENE 4

CARPALIN, ROSETTE, PHILIPIN, LIDAME

CARPALIN: Rosette, this instruction is sufficient for me; I'll know how to take advantage of it, occasionally. But what is wrong with Philipin?

PHILIPIN: God help us, my master-blunderer is a fop without remedy. He met Lidame and entertained her in his foolish manner, according to what he told me, playing the wit.

LIDAME (at the inn's door): Rosette!

ROSETTE: Go away, my mistress calls me. Don't argue, just come to show yourself to her.

LIDAME: Where did she go so late? Rosette!

ROSETTE: Here she is.

LIDAME: Why were you so long in coming.

ROSETTE: I met this unhappy fellow on the road. He told me some details about his life, how ill-favored he is. His master fired him; thus he comes here to offer you his services.

LIDAME: What? His master fired him?

PHILIPIN: He has beaten me, abused me a thousand times, then he fired me without having paid me my wages. Ma'am, it's a hangman. His cruel hand used to give me more strokes than bread. That's the reason why I left him to devote my services to you, lady!

ROSETTE: Don't worry; ma'am will accept your services.

LIDAME: No, I've changed my plan; I would rather refrain.

PHILIPIN: I was sure of such a misfortune. My master warned me, while he was firing me, he would go to see you, ma'am, in order to tell you stories about me. He is able to invent stories in a way to prevent you from hiring me and advising you to keep me away from your daughter, fearing I would have been bribed by some lover to inspire your daughter with some dangerous advice. Thus he would warn you not to trust me or, otherwise, you would soon be abused so much you wouldn't believe it yourself.

LIDAME: These are his words.

PHILIPIN: You see what a dangerous mind he has, that evildoer.

ROSETTE: Ma'am is open-minded and will realize that your master is inspired by animosity.

LIDAME: Actually, your unsophisticated words are for me a proof that your master's veracity cannot be trusted. I'll not believe him and will accept your services in spite of your slyness. As of this moment you are in my service. Cleander will understand through this fact that it's not easy to deceive Lidame.

CARPALIN *(approaching)*: Excuse me, please. For heaven's sake, I heard some news, a name that is dear to me; Lidame is the name. Is she not from Auxerre?

LIDAME: That's right. That's her native land.

CARPALIN: Is she all right?

LIDAME: Yes, sir, thank God.

CARPALIN: Is she there, in her native land?

LIDAME: Oh, no, she's here.

CARPALIN: What do you say! What a joy! Oh, God, please give me the chance to see her!

LIDAME: Here you see her; it's me!

CARPALIN: Is that so? Are you Lidame?

LIDAME: Yes, sir. That's my name.

CARPALIN: Ah, Lidame, sister! Recognize Celidan.

LIDAME: What? My brother Celidan? After thirty years of absence I finally see him?

CARPALIN: Yes, yes, come and hug me. Don't doubt; it's me. You always loved me, since my childhood.

LIDAME: Everybody thought you were dead, and I would cry continually.

CARPALIN: I have remembered your friendship. This remembrance had me come back here. When I had to leave my father's house, after having killed my adversary in a duel, and after I had bid farewell to you, sitting with tears in your eyes, I received ten gold coins from under your straw mattress. Then I went to Dieppe, where I went on board a ship, to enter the American trade. I went through great misery, during long years of hard work, but now I am a wealthy man eager to see my folks. I had my goods transported to this place.

LIDAME: Really, this is a strange adventure.

CARPALIN: I am waiting for the payment of a bill of exchange. I would like to wait patiently in order to spend the rest of my life near my dear sister. I am grateful to the Providence for sending me here. I am greatly at ease and these are my tears of joy. I intend to place my goods under your care.

LIDAME: I have never doubted you loved me.

CARPALIN: I am eager to prove you my love every day. Aren't you married?

LIDAME: I am a widow.

CARPALIN: Too bad! But isn't there a nephew left from this husband of yours?

LIDAME: No, I have only a daughter who is young and beautiful.

CARPALIN: She should get a good husband. All I have will be hers.

PHILIPIN: If someone understands this better, I would be a fool.

LIDAME: Do you want to see her?

CARPALIN: Of course, my sister; please let me see her.

LIDAME: She stays with me in this inn.

CARPALIN: Have her come; you will be better located in my place. I'll show you to my well-furnished lodgings. I'll never leave you until death separates us.

LIDAME: My brother, we'll do anything you like.

ROSETTE: That's not too bad. Carpalin isn't silly.

SCENE 5

COURCAILLET, LIDAME, CARPALIN, ROSETTE, PHILIPIN

COURCAILLET: Ma'am, you may now have supper, according to your order. What shall I prepare?

LIDAME: I'm going to my brother. I don't need anything tonight.

COURCAILLET: Ho, ho, whom do I see here? Strangely enough, it's Carpalin. Sir, what a transformation!

ROSETTE: You are wrong. You don't know this gentleman. He just returned from the West Indies.

COURCAILLET: Wrong. It's an innkeeper. My eyes see quite well.

ROSETTE: You are dreaming; you are dim-sighted.

CARPALIN: Who is this insolent man?

PHILIPIN: That's a good answer.

COURCAILLET: You are well dressed and put on a know-something look.

ROSETTE: You should talk respectfully to Lidame's brother.

COURCAILLET: Oh, that's your brother. Excuse me, ma'am. I thought first he was one of our neighbors. I bet he quite resembles him, but two men can sometimes deceive by their likeness.

LIDAME: Brother, excuse my host's ignorance.

COURCAILLET: Your Grace, please excuse me, I have some problems with my eyes. I'm going to return to my duties.

CARPALIN: I excuse you; go. Sister, let's enter my place; let's hurry up.

LIDAME: Rosette, Philipin, have Lucresse come too.

CARPALIN: My place is at the Golden Lion.

PHILIPIN: Yes, sir. Please go. I know the way to follow you.

SCENE 6

LUCRESSE, PHILIPIN, ROSETTE

LUCRESSE: What can my mother be doing out so late in the street?

PHILIPIN: Here's Lucresse. Welcome! I'm going to look for my master. He's dying to see you. He'll be able to wish you good evening now.

ROSETTE: Hurry! We'll wait for you at the door.

LUCRESSE: But it's late at night.

ROSETTE: Don't worry, the night is a proper time for lovers, who may then speak of their feelings with less shame than during the day.

LUCRESSE: But where are you leading me? I can't understand.

ROSETTE: I'm leading you to Cleander's landlord. He's supposed to be your uncle, and in this false role he's meeting your mother in this house. Ha! Ma'am arrives. I hear her coming down.

SCENE 7

LIDAME, ROSETTE, LUCRESSE

LIDAME: Why don't you come in? What are you waiting for?

LUCRESSE: I don't expect anybody.

LIDAME: You are pretending, but in vain. Who would oblige you to tolerate the fool? My daughter, actually, your mood makes me feel uneasy. I am aware you're coquettish. Your gesture, speech, and manners have confirmed my suspicions this very day. I watched you about twenty times, how you walked to the window to see whether some suitors would appear. If they are well dressed, well sprinkled with powder in the hair, if their bands are well arranged and pulled up, if they have a little moustache and if their trouser legs are covering their round bucklers, that's all of interest to you in this place.

LUCRESSE: What kind of interest would that be?

LIDAME: You are interested in showing your pretty nose, figure, to some young passer-by who may cast amorous glances and come to keep you company, and, in my absence, talk to you. Now go; your uncle wants to see you

LUCRESSE: What? Without you?

LIDAME: Yes, I don't care. Go in. I order it.

LUCRESSE: If . .

LIDAME: Don't say one word more. Go and entertain him. I'll see whether somebody who is supposed to arrive will really come.

LUCRESSE: But . . .

LIDAME: Go in, I tell you!

LUCRESSE *(apart)*: She will see Cleander.

SCENE 8

LIDAME, CLEANDER, PHILIPIN

PHILIPIN: You are awaited at this door.

CLEANDER: Why such a change? You didn't tell me anything about it.

PHILIPIN: Go; it's a success above your understanding.

CLEANDER: Keep aside.

PHILIPIN: That's what I want to do. Between a couple of lovers a third person can be a nuisance only

CLEANDER: Beautiful subject of my passionate love, what words could express my delight in seeing you, my lovely Lucresse?

LIDAME *(aside)*: No doubt, he is mistaken. He will talk about it, and I have to listen to what he'll say.

CLEANDER: What a joy for me to hear that I'm allowed to greet you here tonight. When I am supposed to come to you love gives me wings.

LIDAME: I suspected that; she was waiting for him.

CLEANDER: Lucresse is right and Cleander is in love? This favor has completed my wishes. That's not enough for my love and too much for my merit.

LIDAME: Is that Cleander? Let's see the hypocrite.

CLEANDER: What? You sent for me? This proof of good will is beyond any comparison. My happiness must be visible.

LIDAME: And my shame is obvious. My daughter must have sent word. Oh, what an imprudence!

CLEANDER: My attentions have been too well repaid, and my mind is therefore delighted. No doubt I am loved. It is clear to me that this hot flame of your eyes is received by my soul. I am flattered by this delightful hope.*

---

*Lidame spoke aside. Cleander heard no reply.

LIDAME: No doubt my daughter has been led astray.

CLEANDER: What is the reason for your silence? You don't tell me anything. Are you afraid of your mother? I think she is a simpleton, and I'm clever enough to appease her, even if she surprises us. Would you admire my conduct and her lack of prudence? She respects and trusts me. She's ready to depend upon me to such a degree that she believes all I say like articles of faith. In one word, she is a provincial woman; that means she is common, thoughtless, rough in manners, easy to be duped without noticing it, a person who takes what's false for truth, the white for the black, believing in being refined while she is outwitted.

LIDAME: Very well, very well. This poetry flatters me.

CLEANDER: We don't have to be afraid of her. If she just knew how to put a stop to my transport of joy, at caressing this ivorylike little hand of yours. I can obtain this favor from her, in spite of herself. Yes, whatever she tries to do can be in vain only, and I will be happy to kiss such a beautiful hand.

LIDAME (slapping his face): Yes, you'd kiss it?

CLEANDER: Oh, I have broken teeth.

LIDAME: Your sweet words have to be rewarded in this manner.

CLEANDER: Oh, it's the mother! Oh, ma'am!

LIDAME: Oh, sir! Insolent man, you come here to court the lady! My daughter has a secret passion for you, and you come to spoil her and talk sweet nonsense. Now, you will get acquainted with the fact that honor is precious to me. I'm going to tear out the pupils of your eyes.

CLEANDER: I must escape.

LIDAME: You escape, deceiver; my anger surprises you. Go, you'll not lose a bit of my anger; I have a rod in vinegar for you.

SCENE 9

PHILIPIN, CLEANDER

CLEANDER: Philipin, Philipin

PHILIPIN: Well, what have you done? Do you return full of joy, satisfied? Are you quite positive the beautiful girl loves you?

Did she give you any new proof of love while I was watching over the mule, in this place?

CLEANDER: No, I only received a slap in the face.

PHILIPIN: God save me from such a caress!

CLEANDER: I met here Lidame instead of my mistress.

PHILIPIN: And you immediately talked about your chance and explained yourself well to her?

CLEANDER: Yes, I revealed everything; I exposed my love.

PHILIPIN: Well, well, another case of folly.

CLEANDER: Whoever loves is blind, to a certain degree.

PHILIPIN: You were indiscreet before you fell in love. This bad quality is an inherent evil; it certainly was inherited from your father. Nevertheless, follow me!

CLEANDER: Where do you lead me?

PHILIPIN: Follow me, without any fear or question.

ACT V

SCENE 1

CLEANDER, PHILIPIN, *in a room*

CLEANDER: Where am I? Tell me!

PHILIPIN: In a dark room. Let's get out of here and lock the door up.

CLEANDER: *(alone)*: That's not enough information for me. See? How he kept me alone and locked me up? I cannot leave; he locked the door! God, what does this traitor pretend, doing such a thing? What does this mean? I am retained alone in an unknown place, without any light? What was his purpose in bringing me here? Is it to serve me? Or to do me some harm? What am I supposed to prepare myself for? What have I to be afraid of and wait for? This surprising success seems strange. It's a new labyrinth for my reasoning, I am getting lost. The darkness of this place surrounds both my soul and my eyes. I don't know what to think about, whatever I have in view. Oh, I hear some voice; someone has arrived and I'll get some news.

Scene 2

PHILIPIN, CLEANDER

PHILIPIN: Oh, sir, hurry up, conceal yourself!

CLEANDER: I?

PHILIPIN: Don't discourse; follow me, that's all.

CLEANDER: Why do I have to be hidden? Ha, actually, I don't care.

PHILIPIN: But, your life is at stake, sir!

CLEANDER: I don't care; don't think they will get my life easily. If I were hidden people would think I am guilty.

PHILIPIN: A light is approaching. People will surprise you. Think about getting hidden somewhere.

CLEANDER (taking his sword out): I think about defending myself.

Scene 3

ROSETTE, LUCRESSE, CLEANDER, PHILIPIN

ROSETTE: Ma'am, let's escape. I see a thief.

LUCRESSE: No, it's Cleander . . .

CLEANDER: Ah! Lucresse!

LUCRESSE: What a misfortune! I came up to this room, ordered to do so by my mother. She wants to talk to me. She is very angry.

CLEANDER: Why in this room?

PHILIPIN: Don't talk so much. Her mother is going to come here. Hide yourself right away!

LUCRESSE: Hurry up, for Heaven's sake! It seems to me she's coming. Go . .

CLEANDER (entering a closet): I would die rather than understand anything of all this humbug.

Scene 4

LIDAME, ROSETTE, LUCRESSE, CLEANDER, PHILIPIN

LUCRESSE: Why does he close the door? I am shaking. Ma'am, what's wrong?

LIDAME: How dare you ask this question? Ungrateful and shameful daughter, your love brings to shame an illustrious family.

LUCRESSE: I? Would you kindly explain this to me better?

LIDAME: Oh, look at this insolent girl, how she dares to reply! You impudent woman, you plan to abuse me and pretend to be ignorant. Any dissimulation is unnecessary now since I know everything.

LUCRESSE: What?

LIDAME: Your plotting, from one end to the other. Your secret dates, your love for Cleander, and everything this traitor has dared to undertake for you. I caught him in the very act, this mean-spirited deceiver.

PHILIPIN (*in the closet*): We are discovered, sir. I am practically dead of fear.

LIDAME: It's time now to answer me.

LUCRESSE: I don't know what to say. What you said is enough to mix me up. Yes, know, Cleander came to see me.

LIDAME: In this regard I know all that can be known. I'll not let his audacity remain unpunished. An attack on my honor is an attack on my life.

PHILIPIN: We have to be comforted! I haven't succeeded too well! But if I am beaten you will be beaten as well!

LIDAME: A dagger I carry, being mad with rage, in this justified case, will show how I reject an outrage and will make this man understand how much a mad woman should be feared. This dagger will kill him and he'll die pierced by it.

PHILIPIN: Oh, I see her tinged with blood. Fie, it's a little nothing, but it always makes me shiver more and more.

LUCRESSE: Ma'am! Please calm down, you have a furious plan.

Actually, Cleander is hidden in this place. His safety and his fall depend entirely upon you.

LIDAME: Heaven! What a misfortune have I discovered!

LUCRESSE: I don't dare denying all you know so well.

LIDAME: I know it now, but I didn't know it before. He will not escape, this perfidious traitor!

PHILIPIN: My master, go first; this honor belongs to you.

LIDAME: Where can he be concealed? Let's look for him carefully!

LUCRESSE: I could inform you, without further research.

LIDAME: Speak, hurry!

LUCRESSE: Since I have to inform you, I will tell you. He is hidden at the bottom of my heart. Yes, here he is triumphant, my lover, a charming man; he is charmed by myself as much as he charms me. You may beat him here, if you want. Love has interwoven his fate with my life. This dear man who displeases you so much will die with me.

LIDAME: What have I heard? Unfortunate girl! You have a suitor? You are in love? Cleander is the master of your heart, you say? Are you not afraid of my anger? I knew; here is still another mystery!

LUCRESSE: If I am a criminal, at least I am sincere. Yes, Cleander occupies the first place in my heart, and I prefer to die if I cannot live for him.

LIDAME: What you just told me doesn't comfort me. Your reason goes astray; you talk like a fool. This evil comes from your novel-reading; you just memorize the words of nice feelings expressed sweetly, learn all about the gentle meetings and the artifice that usually brings girls to be dishonored. Change! Change your life or, I promise you, you'll never be the beneficiary of my goods. Don't date Cleander or you will lose everything.

LUCRESSE: His family belongs to the nobility and is easy to deal with. He wants to marry me.

LIDAME: Believe me, I would rather have you enter a convent. I know how to keep you safe from Cleander, you impertinent girl! Since this affair is quite important, I'm going to my brother to ask for his advice. I'll do everything he advises and will not do anything without his agreement.

PHILIPIN: She is leaving. Now, everything will be all right.

CLEANDER *(sneezes)*: Ha, ha.

PHILIPIN: Sir, what's wrong? God bless your heart!

LIDAME: What kind of noise did I hear?

CLEANDER: Oh, my misfortune! What did I do!

LIDAME: Who was sneezing in this closet?

LUCRESSE: I haven't heard anything, who could that be?

LIDAME: The excuse is bad, and my hearing is good. With some light I'll be able to see.

LUCRESSE: Oh, Cleander is discovered. I am desperate. Ma'am, stop. Give me this candle. Rosette will keep it.

LIDAME: I don't need her.

PHILIPIN *(leaving the closet)*: I have to dupe her once more, in spite of her teeth.

LIDAME: Ho, ho, it's Philipin. What did you do in this closet?

PHILIPIN: This full light hurts my eyes. I'm dazzled. Please put out this light.

LIDAME: What are you doing here at this hour?

PHILIPIN: Oh, ma'am, it's you! Excuse me, please. I am not able to use an artifice. I used to sleep like a top. After dinner, being a little tired, I became drowsy in an armchair, where I snored, as usual, like in a bed. Then, sneezing, I woke up, after about an hour of sleep. According to Albert, who, some time ago was an authority, if you get up in such a way, it's a bad foreboding. To tell you the truth, I was worrying about this sneezing.

LIDAME: Will you still dare to give the lie to your mother? "Nobody was sneezing; this is a vain imagination." Thank God, my judgment is sound and I am not easily deceived. I don't like what you do, and I'm going to my brother to warn him about it.

CLEANDER *falls and makes some stools fall as well*

CLEANDER: She is leaving. Let's go out. Heaven! What a misfortune; how unhappy am I!

LIDAME: What do I hear now?

ROSETTE: Your master, Philipin, is short of brains.

PHILIPIN: Should we be surprised? Is it something new?

LIDAME: Who can make so much noise in this closet?

PHILIPIN: When I was sleeping, maybe someone introduced himself there. I'm going to check, right away. I'll avenge it myself. Someone needs your goods.

LIDAME: It's Cleander, this cowardly suborner who wants to dishonor me, and with me the whole honorable family.

PHILIPIN: Ma'am, if it's really he, his intended deed will be punished by death. If my body is short, my courage is great. Give me this dagger and the light and, in order to avoid any accident, follow me. He will pay for his deed much more than people pay at the marketplace. If I don't find him he must have been well hidden.

LIDAME: Go; your loyalty will be rewarded.

PHILIPIN *(falls and blows the light out)*: Help!

LIDAME: What's wrong with you?

PHILIPIN: I broke my scalp. As soon as I entered here I saw a giant. Filled with fear, I had a horrible impression. He appeared to me as a giant. His terrible arm gave me a blow and, like a thunderbolt, he made my nose touch the soil, blowing my light out. If he had repeated it I would have been crushed completely. This must have been a ghost. If you are prudent, you will not remain here any longer.

LUCRESSE: I'm afraid of ghosts, ma'am. Let's go away

LIDAME: This one shouldn't scare you. Your eagerness shows me that it's a trick. I know it's Cleander, and Philipin is mistaken.

PHILIPIN: I don't say no; I may be mistaken. But, in case it's Cleander, he cannot escape.

LIDAME: Then, don't leave me alone.

PHILIPIN: I'll be very faithful.

LIDAME: Rosette, go and look for a candle.

LUCRESSE: May Cleander come out if it's dark? Don't go . . .

ROSETTE: That's well said, I'm going to warn him. (TO CLEANDER) Do you know it's time?

CLEANDER: That's what I am going to do.

LIDAME (*stopping him*): He is caught, the suitor.

CLEANDER: How contrary my fate is to me.

PHILIPIN: You are holding Philipin; don't be mistaken. Hang it! How rude your arm is holding mine!

LIDAME: What? That's you, Philipin? I am embarrassed by this success. I thought to get a hold of this scoundrel, instead of you.

PHILIPIN: God, if it were true, heaven would have delivered into your hands this cowardly suborner.

LIDAME (*taking* CLEANDER's *hand for the second time*): This time, I think I got hold of him.

CLEANDER: You are keeping Philipin.

PHILIPIN: God, what an impertinence.

LIDAME: The trick is rude. I know his voice well.

PHILIPIN: Yes, you hold Cleander. This time he is taken.

LIDAME: A thief, a thief. Quickly, give me a candle.

LUCRESSE: Now, everything is lost, Rosette. What a cruel misfortune!

LIDAME: He tries to escape.

PHILIPIN: No, no, don't worry. I am holding his arm and will stop him.

LIDAME: To keep him from taking off hold him by his long moustache.

PHILIPIN: That's good advice. You are happy. Now go away and leave us your hair.

CLEANDER: (*leaving some hair in* LIDAME's *and* PHILIPIN's *hands*): Here I am freed in a strange manner.

LIDAME: Hey, my brother, hey, friends, bring some light. Finally you're caught, you villain, cowardly lover! Don't think I'll be shamefully crushed, without a punishment for you. There isn't any power in the world that could free you from my justified anger! You cheat, you'll die, and your spilled blood will soon join the loss of my honor.

CLEANDER: God, how hard it is to find the door! I had better remain hidden here, since a light is being brought.

Scene 5 (The Last)

CARPALIN, LIDAME, LUCRESSE, ROSETTE, CLEANDER

CARPALIN: Where is he hidden, this swindler-thief?

LIDAME: Heaven, what do I hold? What do I see? I'll die of sadness.

PHILIPIN: I never saw, in my whole life, anything so ludicrous.

LUCRESSE: Cleander escaped. God, I'm delighted.

CARPALIN: What a sudden fright has stricken you? I don't see anything.

LIDAME: The traitor escaped.

CARPALIN: Who?

LIDAME: The suborner, called Cleander, who has seduced your niece.

CARPALIN: I'll have him be hanged.

PHILIPIN: We were holding him by his hair, but all our efforts were in vain; all he left us is a tuft of his hair.

CARPALIN: On my word, only his death would have paid for the outrage. Why didn't I keep him here myself, this perfidious impostor? It would be a pleasure for me to eat up his heart, to devour this insolent traitor. We should look for him everywhere; he may be hidden here somewhere

LIDAME: Just before you came he went down.

PHILIPIN: If I can find him, believe me he'll be lost.

CLEANDER *(in the closet)*: I must keep my sword ready for use, in case of necessity. Is that Carpalin or is my sight now wrong?

CARPALIN: He isn't here. Sir, don't say a word. I am working for you; don't be a fool. Before the light was brought here he must have escaped.

LIDAME: I knew it. You, my shameless daughter, your mind is vile, and you cherish your error! Don't expect my feelings to be tender. I do not wish to have such a weak daughter. Any mild feelings are now thrown out of my heart. I don't recognize her as my descendant, since she has tarnished her good name. Go, I have disowned you, and tomorrow you will be confined in an austere convent.

CARPALIN: I think it would be better to have her taste the fruit of marriage in order to save her honor and to appease you, since she fell in love and is of age. That may prevent any evil from happening. Often honor is lost if you try too hard to maintain it.

LIDAME: That would be all right if he were not so impossible. Who else would want her after such an insult? Lisipe is fond of her, but when he returns and is informed about her weakness, his love will vanish. Who would take a body whose soul belongs to another man? Who would marry her?

CLEANDER *(leaving the closet)*: It will be me, ma'am. Please concede her to me.

PHILIPIN: Oh, here's the shuffler. Was there ever a sillier lover?

LIDAME: Ah, here's the impostor! His love is offensive to us. Have him die. I expect you to avenge the affront.

CLEANDER: I am taking your daughter.

LIDAME: My daughter is not a game for a hunting swindler.

CARPALIN: Let him talk about his folks and his wealth. Then we may decide whether he should marry her or die.

LIDAME: It's not too bad to try mildness, my brother.

CLEANDER: Your brother?

LIDAME: Yes, I'm his sister.

CLEANDER: You may do without this trick. I do not refuse this adorable girl for my wife. To have me accept this proposal you did not need a brother—impostor.

LIDAME: He really is my brother.

CLEANDER: He is an impostor. Excuse my frankness, but I have the habit of speaking frankly.

CARPALIN *(to PHILIPIN)*: Your master loses his reason.

PHILIPIN: Reason? Is that a mockery? How could he lose it; he never had any.

LIDAME: Do you know him?

CLEANDER: I am supposed to know him pretty well.

CARPALIN: Don't believe the words of a traitor.

CLEANDER: Look at this disguised man. Who wouldn't know him? I'm not so stupid as everybody believes.

LIDAME: What do I hear? From one evil I am falling into another one.

PHILIPIN *(to* CLEANDER*)*: Your tongue destroys us all.

CLEANDER: I cannot deny it. All these disguises will not be good for anything. I am not mistaken; I know this man well.

CARPALIN: Oh, you know me, what an extravagance! Where could you have seen me? In New France?

CLEANDER: Not at all

CARPALIN: Thus I don't know where. In California? In Brazil? In Peru? In Protopotossy? In Lima? In Cumane? In Chica? In Cusco? In Tolme-Caribane?

CLEANDER: Do we need so much fuss, we two? Do you think I'll be surprised by these savage names?

CARPALIN: These are the places where I've spent my life.

CLEANDER: You never left your inn.

CARPALIN: Speak better, you indiscreet lover!

CLEANDER: That's too much! This man is the innkeeper; his name is Carpalin. I live in his inn. You should believe me.

LIDAME: What? You live in his inn?

CLEANDER: Yes it's the inn called the Black Head.

LIDAME: How do you explain this, impostor?

CARPALIN: Oh, ma'am, stop. I'm going to tell you many other truthful secrets. Rosette, Philipin, and even your daughter are involved in this stratagem. I too play a part in it.

LIDAME: My daughter?

CARPALIN: The intention was good.

LUCRESSE: I confessed to you, my mother, my love for Cleander. I allowed this man to play the role as an impostor to make you well disposed toward my marriage.

CARPALIN: Ma'am, believe me, you could have been worse related. He is the only son of Du Bailly de Nogent.

LIDAME: I forgive you everything if he is really the son of such a man. My late husband loved him like a brother.

CLEANDER: He doesn't own many goods.

LIDAME: He is an honorable man. In such a misfortune that's a happy issue. From now on, Lucresse may love you without being scolded. My declaration makes her love legitimate. My daughter, you may love Cleander as your husband.

LUCRESSE: No order was ever sweeter than this one.

CLEANDER: To make our pleasure still more perfect, let's marry up Philipin and Rosette, together with our wedding.

CARPALIN: And what shall I be?

CLEANDER: We are generous. You comforted us, and we'll make you happy

ROSETTE: Philipin, what do you say to all this?

PHILIPIN: What do you want me to say? I think I see the happy end of a comedy.

ROSETTE: I'm still afraid regarding your master. I'm shaking secretly.

PHILIPIN: The comedy has ended. He is no longer indiscreet.

Part II
BARBIERI'S INAVVERTITO
AND MOLIERE'S BLUNDERER,
AN ESSAY IN
COMPARATIVE LITERATURE

INTRODUCTORY NOTE

After studying Quinault's *The Indiscreet Lover, or The Master Blunderer* the student should read Molière's comedy in verse *The Blunderer, or The Counterplots,* in any translation. For my essay in comparative literature, following on the next pages, I used the edition of Ernest Rhys, preceded by the introduction of Frederick C. Grees, Everyone's Library (New York, 1929),[1] included in volume I. Any other translation may serve for the student's interest as well.

My essay takes into consideration both comedies, Molière's *Blunderer* and Barbieri's *L'Inavvertito*. It is supposed to be used as a demonstration of methods in comparative literature. It may serve the student to do a similar essay comparing Quinault's *Indiscreet Lover* with Barbieri's *Inavvertito,* then the Dryden comedy, as mentioned before and later. In order to facilitate this work some questions and suggestions are added at the end of this part.

The student may choose other methods, under his adviser's guidance. The essay is only one of many methods that can be used in comparative literature. It may be useful or replaced by other analytical research, or completed by a historical or other

method. Our goals in comparative literature are intended to give
a motivation to the student. He may be motivated to choose an
analysis according to his own understanding. The final motive
may be to find out whether it is important for the comparatist to
determine who has used the comedy of the other author as a
source of inspiration. Since we tend rather to appreciate the originality of authors who added some precious works to the common
treasure of the world's masterpieces or works deserving attention,
the analogies should not be the core of our research; it should
center around the author's genius in inventing or depicting his
own world, rather than around imitation or plagiarism—words
that did not exist, in the modern sense, in the seventeenth century.

A. THE COMMON THEME AND THE CHARACTERS

The title *L'Inavvertito* appeared in Taschereau's edition of
Molière's Works in French, in its original Italian, according to the
Italian edition of 1650: *Inavvertito, overo Scappino disturbato
e Mezzetino travagliato. Commedia di Nicolo Barbieri detto Bel-
trame . . . in Venetia. MDCXXX. Per Angelo Salvatori, Librario
à S. Moïse.*

In my Essay I used this Italian text as printed in Taschereau's
edition preceding Molière's *Blunderer* in its French text.

THE COMMON THEME

In both comedies there is a lover who mars all the tricks of
his servant; a servant whose tricks are intended to secure his master's happiness; two rivals in love with the same girl, Celia; the
protagonist's father who wants to marry his son to another girl
from a good family who is in love with another man, one of the
rivals. The protagonist is portrayed as a little silly, conceited,
believing in his own wit, but, convinced by his servant of the
contrary, relies entirely on his servant's slyness.

THE CHARACTERS
(in order as they may serve for comparison)

Molière's *Blunderer*	Barbieri's *Inavvertito*
Lelio, son to Pandolphus	*Fulvio,* son to Pantalone
Leander, a young gentleman of good birth (I rival)	*Cintio,* a scholar (first rival)
Anselmo, an old man (Hippolyta's father)	*Beltrame,* Lavinia's father
Andrès, a supposed gipsy (II rival)	*Captain Bellorofonte Martelione,* a stranger (second rival)
Mascarille, servant to Lelio	*Scappino,* servant to Fulvio
Ergaste, a servant (Mascarille's friend)	*Spacca,* Scappino's friend
Two Troupes of Masqueraders	
Celia, slave to Trufaldin	*Celia,* slave to Mezzetino, a merchant of slaves
Trufaldin, a refugee whose true name is Zanobio Ruberti	*Mezzetino*

From this list of characters we may already figure out the analogies of the plot: The servant helps his master to get Celia, eliminating all those who are in his way to his master's happiness.

B. THE ANALOGIES

The names in both comedies are mainly Italian. Molière used names like Lelio, Anselmo, Celia, and the place of his comedy is Messina, in Sicily.

Farcical comical devices, such as beating on stage and a comical intervention of the police, belong to details used frequently since the Middle Ages. More psychological comical devices used in both comedies are mutual confidences made by the rivals (*Inavv.* I,1), implied in *The Blunderer* (I,1 and 2). We hear that Lelio is aware of Leander's love for Celia; his rival must have told him about it before the play starts. Such confidences among lovers who are not too smart to conceal anything are observed from life. The servants, Scappino and Mascarille, pretend to be ready to enter the service of another master, the rival No. I, in order to find out the rival's plans for getting to Celia.

The boasting about one's own wit is a known comical device from the Attic comedy, found in Plautus's comedies *(Formio)*, and, as we know, Plautus was a translator of Attic comedies. The Italian boasting character, the Capitano, was a preferred type of the *commedia dell'arte,* and the Braggart was a beloved motive of French farces and monologues,[2] especially those attributed to the fifteenth and sixteenth centuries. Braggarts were known as boasting about love, military achievements, or adventures. The Blunderer, in both comedies, thinks he is a witty fellow easily outwitting his servant. Actually it is just the contrary, as his servant seeks to convince him.

The scolding of the master by his servant, the ever-renewed tricks of a different character by the servant, mostly corresponding to the climax of each act, in both comedies (five acts, five main tricks), comical situations of discovered disguised characters by the master for whom they were disguised, and foreign words, comical mispronounced words of their own language, as well as barbarisms and solecisms are analogical in both comedies, while they are used in a way to flatter the taste of the public of each country differently. Thus Barbieri used Latin quotations, like *Lasciate la cura ame. De mandato curiae Vicariae* (Act III,4); mispronounced French and Spanish words, like *furbarie,* instead of *fourberie,* as pronounced in Venice, sse-endings instead of sce-endings, as in a Venetian dialect (see the editor's note, page 245 and other notes on the following pages), and Scappino's advice to Spacca: "You have to play so that Pantalone believes that you are a stranger" (IV,3); i.e., what is strange, foreign, is comical. The Captain is a "stranger" from Sicily. As we know from history, Sicily was a separate kingdom that got the name of *Kingdom of Two Sicilies* in 1442, which disappeared only in 1861, absorbed by the new kingdom of Italy. In the seventeenth century Sicily was a foreign country, and the Capitano was considered a "stranger" to the Italian country and society. In IV,6 the Captain asks: "Can you recognize a gentleman according to his appearance?" Mezzetino answers: "Sir, I find that men are like watermelons that deceive not only through their appearance, but even through their weight and smell." In other words, Italians cannot recognize a foreign gentleman through his appearance; they do not know what personality is covered by the appearance. In the list of characters, the Captain is a *forestiero* (stranger). A funny superlative is made from the word meaning policeman, *birro*, when Mezzetino wants to flatter the policeman, calling him *"birrissimo"* (II,14), and the Philippines serve to make *filippinando* (in Scene 4).

Molière's use of foreign words is difficult to judge in a translated text, but even in the translated *Blunderer* we find that for Molière everything foreign was amusing. In Act III,5, the guidelines are taken from "Olibrius, the slayer of the innocents, who, as explained in Note 18, was a Roman governor of Gaul, at the time of Emperor Decius, known as very cruel, and as a great boaster." The action is placed in Messina, and Trufaldin's past is related to Naples. Some of Mascarille's tricks refer to Turkey, etc. Mascarille is disguised as a Swiss (V,4). Both gipsies, Celia and Andrès, are involved in a strange *quiproquo*. Lelio recognizes Mascarille under his grotesque dress (V,7), and the servant answers him in his gibberish,*"Moi non point Masquerille"* (Note 28), i.e., "I am not Masquerille" (*Mascarille* means a female pander), just mispronouncing his own name ridiculously. The two old women, toward the end of the comedy, fight a furious combat, not shown on stage but narrated in a grotesque comical humor by Mascarille (final scenes). In Act II, Scene 11, Mascarille calls himself *regum imperator,* i.e., emperor of rogues, rascals, in Latin.

The tradition of using foreign words, dialects, solecisms, and barbarisms in French literature is well known before Molière. The French *Farce of the Worthy Master Pathelin* has the protagonist pronounce strange words sounding like dialects or foreign words, when he is lying in bed, and the merchant arrives to claim payment. Rabelais has his Panurge introduced to Pantagruel, for the first time, as a student of foreign languages; and allusions to English in French farces and sotties are too numerous to be quoted.

Some analogies may be found in using comical gestures, seen by the master, misinterpreted by him when his servant wants to prevent him from marring everything again, and causing the master's anger, in both comedies. Much is left to the acting artists; thus we cannot judge today how it was played in the seventeenth century. Other analogies may be found by student-professor investigations, but it is not important to pay much attention to analogies if our goal is to find out the playwright's originality.

C. ORIGINALITY

Barbieri is supposed to have depicted his characters from life, partly from former classical comedies. In his *Prologo*, Barbieri first writes about comedies, in general, their goal being to teach and raise people, then about the difference between comedy and life. Comedy, according to Barbieri, teaches us how good can be derived from evil, not the contrary. In a comedy, devices are detested, stealing by servants is punished, avarice and silly love affairs of old men are ridiculed, and everything ends for the best. But, since characters are represented by comedians, critics reject comedy in a golden oratory manner. Such is the destiny of telling stories, and such is the world. Authority disguises faults and has them appear in form of virtues. If a gentleman says ridiculous words he is considered facetious, but if a simple man does the same he will be called a buffoon. If a rich man says satirical words, he will be called "witty spirit," but if a poor man does the same, he will be backbitten. If a nobleman is boring his companion, he will be judged a man of humor, but if a commoner does so, he will be considered insolent. If an eminent man invites himself frequently to his acquaintances, he will be affable, but if an ordinary man does the same, he will be called a freeloader. If a respectable man disregards etiquette at dinner, he will be accepted by the company as a man who dislikes formalities, but if a not highly educated man does the same, he will be called a villain. In short, false gems in the hand of a chevalier will pass for precious stones, but if diamonds are in the hands of a poor man, they will be considered false stones. As for me, Barbieri says, I believe that the comedy of today deserves more appreciation. It is necessary to divert people from vices. I affirm that they have honest intentions. What I stated is the truth; such is the approach of the society to men. Here is one proof, the style of modern comedies. Please condescend to pay attention to it.

In *L'Inavvertito* Barbieri has his spokesman, Scappino, say several statements that recall these words from the *Prologo*. In Act I,10, Scappino says to Lavinia, "If you do a thing it will be appreciated, not so if I do the same thing. If your father will bring Celia into your house there will be an opportunity to bring together Fulvio and Celia." *Lavinia:* "Wouldn't you call such a procedure a kind of go-between?" *Scappino:* "With regard to a person like me this word would be used. If a gentleman does the same thing, people used to say that he is doing a favor; regarding a lady they would say that she is helpful. Ruffianism is like stealing. If it is done by a statesman . . . , " etc.

Molière did not write a prologue to his *Blunderer,* but understood that comedy has to teach through laughter, as he expressed it later. Mascarille makes remarks about social appreciation according to the social status of the person who did something. In Act I,2, Mascarille says, "When people have need of us, poor servants, we are darlings and incomparable creatures; but at other times, at the least fit of anger, we are scoundrels and ought to be soundly thrashed." The social status is more balanced in Molière's play; not only the master beats the servant, but the servant beats the master as well (IV,8). The vision of the society is more positive in Molière's comedy than in Barbieri's *Inavver-*

tito. Celia in the *Blunderer* is a modest, spiritual girl who does not want to injure anybody, is witty, knows how to conceal the plan, and gives Mascarille the information he needs for Lelio. In Act I,3 when asked whether she dabbles in the black art, as a gipsy, she answers that her skill lies entirely in the white, i.e., that she dealt with beneficial spirits.

Lelio, in spite of being impetuous and marring all the tricks of his servant, intended for his good and for Celia's liberation from slavery, is essentially honest. In Act I, Scene 7, he takes up the purse Mascarille had let fall to the ground on purpose, in order to take care of the money in it, and gives it to the owner, Anselmo. He also saves Andrès from jail, where Mascarille had the gipsy imprisoned, on the change of robbery. Mascarille, in Act IV, Scene 8, says in a monologue, "A great robbery has lately been committed, by whom, nobody knows. These gipsies have not generally the reputation of being very honest; upon this slight suspicion, I will cleverly get the fellow imprisoned for a few days. I know some officers of justice, open to a bribe, . . . " Andrès is grateful. In the last scene of the play, he says to Lelio that he repays the obligation (for having been saved by Lelio from jail) by giving him Celia for his wife.

Molière likes to portray his characters through contrast. The honest Lelio is silly, but conceited and, according to Mascarille, possessed by an evil spirit. His contrast, Mascarille, goes his ways in order to defeat his master's bad fortune. His honesty is not an absolute honesty, rather circumstantial. His truth is a truth under circumstantial variety, a particular truth. His cunning wit is expressed through his stratagems, not conforming to our absolute concept of honesty. Thus Molière portrays the two extremes of the society: the sly foxy servant opposed to the silly dreamer of love, honest but marring everything that could bring him profit, both speaking two opposite languages, the language of financial profit (Mascarille) and words of the straight man, believing in Heaven's help, his servant's genius in his service, and in love, *The Blunderer* (Lelio).

Around these two men, main representatives of the society, are other characters, such as Hippolyta, an objective critic of herself and an admirer of Celia's beauty, in spite of the fact that

Celia has captured Leander's admiration, and Hippolyta's love for Leander; the three old men, ridiculed, each one representing another type of the society: Anselmo is an old fool who is naive enough to believe Mascarille's flatteries about Nerina's love for him (I,6). Pandolphus represents the common sense of old men. He accepts the news about his pretended death with good humor, suspects Mascarille's stratagems for the purpose of getting money, and lays information against him with the police. The third old man, Trufaldin, represents the fugitives of their participation in a rebellion in the past and living under a new name, in another place. The past has its impact on his fate, and Zanobio Ruberti, alias Trufaldin, a suspicious tutor of a young slave, finds out that this young lady is his own daughter he wanted to sell. Every complication finally ends happily, not thanks to the shrewd tricks of the cunning servant Mascarille, but by chance, or through Heaven's intervention. Every Jack has his Jill; even Mascarille will find a wife through the help of Andrès, the supposed-to-be gipsy, but actually Horatio, Zanobio's son.

The interest of the play grows by the ingenious tricks, always renewed, in which even Lelio is involved. While Barbieri leaves his blunderer completely unaware of his servant's tricks, Molière has his Lelio play his part in some tricks, but he plays them badly, so that he rather mars all.

Molière suppressed parts of *L'Inavvertito*, added certain episodes, like Lelio's participation in Mascarille's tricks, regrouped scenes and details, and provided an end depending not on sly tricks, but on the past having an impact on the present, probably through God's justice. In spite of many critics who blame the end for not being interesting, we have to take into consideration that this was Molière's first comedy and that his genius was not yet in full development.

The dialogue is voluble and appropriate to the characters who speak. Victor Hugo declared the *dialogue* of *l'Etourdi* to be the best Molière ever wrote.[3]

Barbieri's dialogue is more vivacious. Parts of many scenes are parodies of the classical *stichomythia*, used in Greek tragedies and in pseudo-classical tragicomedies to express an altercation between the speakers in the form of one-line questions, answers, and even half-lines in some Greek tragedies. The best example is the last (thirteenth) scene of the last act (V) of *L'Inavvertito*, where the protagonist does not dare to say yes to his father, who asks him whether he wants to marry Celia. The "master" is so certain that he mars all that he is in a quandary about what to say and looks for his servant to give him permission to say yes to his father. The short lines correspond to the Italian rhythm of speaking and are not so dependent upon the psychology of the characters as Molière's dialogue.

Molière's scene is set in Sicily, but could be anywhere. The place is not important, while *L'Inavvertito* has a certain dependency upon the Italian neighborhood of the sea, since Celia is supposed to go on the ship, and since the Capitano is a stranger.

The portrayal of the servant in *L'Inavvertito* follows to some extent some servants who help their masters like friends in the comedies of Plautus, Terence, and their imitators. Scappino is original in his reasons given to Spacca for always trying to invent new stratagems: every time his master fails, and mars all that the servant has planned and almost achieved his goal, Scappino invents a new trick because he likes his master (he had reared from childhood), and because Scappino is ambitious and wants to improve his master's bad luck. He is portrayed as a simpler, comical edition of Machiavelli.

Scappino is ambitious, thinks about honor and has his own ideas about the world's appreciation: when Spacca states that Scappino wants to finish with honor (Act V, Scene 3), Scappino declares: "Do you think that military stratagems are a knavery? They are considered honorable. Happy is he who through his cunning wit is able to fight and to win battles. He is more appreciated than if he caused a bloody battle." Spacca calls this kind of idea rhetoric.

Mascarille is younger.[4] He has not reared his master but wants to become his tutor and asks for the father's consent and an additional salary. Molière may have thought of the poet François Villon in tracing Mascarille's character. Just as Villon paid tribute to rogues, but was afraid of jail, Mascarille, says, in a soliloquy (Act III, Scene 1), "If I should now give way to my just impatience the world will say I sank under difficulties, that my cunning was completely exhausted. What then becomes of that public esteem, which extols you everywhere as a first-rate rogue, and which you have acquired upon so many occasions, because you never yet were found wanting in inventions? Honor, Mascarille, is a fine thing; do not pause in your noble labors; and whatever a master may have done to incense you, complete your work, for your own glory, and not to oblige him. . . . Well, once more, out of kindness . . . let us take some pains, even if they are in vain."

Here we have a proof that Mascarille is not working, like Scappino, out of love for his master, but thinks about the world's judgment of himself, a first-rate rogue, and wants to be kind to his master. He is afraid of jail, being aware of the fact that he is a rogue (Act V, end of Scene 2), and that his trick of pretending that Pandolphus has passed away may be the cause of his imprisonment: "I am afraid that if I am once housed at the expense of the king, I may like it so well after the first quarter of an hour, that I shall find it very difficult afterwards to get away. There have been several warrants out against me this good while; for virtue is always envied and persecuted in this abominable age" (Act III, Scene 5).

As Villon wanted to be praised by the posterity as a hero, Mascarille says: "Je veux quel'on s'apprête / A me peindre en héros, un laurier sur la tête, / et qu'au bas du portrait on mette en lettres d'or: / *Vivat Mascarillus, fourbûm imperator.* ("I desire that due preparations be made to paint me as a hero crowned with laurel, and that underneath the portrait be inscribed in letters of gold: *Vivat Mascarillus, fourbûm imperator.*")

Thus Molière's servant is original, painted from life, probably from the personality of the fifteenth-century poet François Villon, a witty young man, imprisoned and freed several times.

D. QUESTIONS

These questions for students of comparative literature, regarding Molière's *Blunderer* and Quinault's *Indiscreet Lover* are to be answered either according to the preceding essay, or individually, or strictly according to the questions.

Before we start giving questions and answers we should be fully aware of the fact that critical approaches to works of literary art have changed during the last two centuries. While, at the time of Sainte-Beuve, biography was considered extremely important and questions of who was first to write about something were at the core of research, our contemporary approach to works of literary art is different. In 1909 Marcel Proust wrote his essay *Contre Sainte-Beuve,* which was published in 1954 and which changed the outlook in criticism completely. First of all, it is not the author who is important, but his work; it is not his life as recalled by friends and relatives that interests us, but his vision of life that is essential. We judge the author and evaluate his work not on the basis of our contemporary ideas, but according to his vision of life in his time. The characters he portrayed are social types, they have been formed by time, environment, and the author's perception of life through his intuition. The basis of research should not be the author's weakness, but his strength in literary art, the originality of his genius. Consequently, for a student of comparative literature the essential study should be devoted to the author's originality.

As a matter of fact, the best work, or works, of the author may not be representative of his art; more important is a comparative analysis of how he developed from the time of his first work to his full mastery. Thus Molière's *Blunderer* is considered to be his first comedy. It would be interesting to find out how his art developed from *The Blunderer* to his great comedies in five acts, like *The Misanthrope,* or others. Quinault's works were not very much appreciated by critics of his time, but there were jealous people among playwrights who did not like his popularity. Wouldn't it be great fun to find out whether his comedies deserve oblivion? People who saw his comedy *The Indiscreet Lover* returned several times to see it, to enjoy its humor and the play of the comedians, as mentioned by several editors.[5]

In the following questions and answers our main attention will be devoted to the vision of the society with characters portrayed from life, and to the national color added by the author for the enjoyment of his public.

1. Questions concerning the comparison between Quinault's and Molière's comedies under consideration:

ANALOGIES
a. The common theme.
b. The common motive of confidences of the two rivals.
c. The common situations of surprise with the arrival of the least-expected person.
d. Scolding scenes in both comedies. Who scolds whom? Who is the actual master? Reproaches.
e. Disguises. Their revelation, unmasking the truth.
f. Empty house to be used for the lovers.
g. Servant of two master-rivals.

ORIGINALITIES

a. *Characters*:
   Which one of the two lovers, Molière's Lelio or Quinault's Cleander, is more realistically portrayed? Lelio, sometimes having to play a role in his servant's plotting, has to learn it by heart; Cleander is never informed what kind of a trick his servant plans to use for his plotting. Consequently, which one seems more realistic? How is it in the Italian comedy? Trufaldin vs. Lidame and Lisipe: does Trufaldin believe the story of his family right away? Does he make inquiries? Compare the attitude of Quinault's characters. How many lines are sufficient to have Lisipe and Lidame accept the news about the pretended truth? If we accept the character of Lisipe as comical, intended by the author to amuse the public through his eagerness to leave Lucresse under the care of his rival, shall we not hesitate to accept a lover's carelessness as possibly true? Lidame too believes the news, first about her brother, then about Cleander, whom she finally accepts as a future son-in-law without questions. She simply accepts him as the son of "such a father." Psychologically speaking, is this a sufficient motivation, after having heard her opposite

words in former situations? Which world seems more realistic?

b. *The Tricks:*
Compare the tricks in Molière's and in Quinault's plays and make a conclusion as to which present more affinity with the preceding ones? Are the stratagems of the servant related? They usually fail, but is the reason for the failure always the same in both plays? What are the aspects of this failure in each comedy? Is there a continuity of trick and surprise through unmasking? In which comedy does each trick assure a better link between the acts?

c. *The Conciseness:*
Where are more characters portrayed? Are Molière's "Two Troupes of Masqueraders" necessary to the plot? In Molière's *Blunderer* eleven characters are listed, besides the Masqueraders. How many does Quinault introduce? Is the role of the police necessary to the plot? Besides the police what has Quinault suppressed in his play? Compare the device of kidnapping, ring, letters. What conclusion do you reach?

d. *Movement:*
Where do we find more movement on stage? Where are the scenes shorter, thus causing persons to come and go more often? Where are the gestures of having the purse fall, holding a character, weeping, laughing, etc., better indicated? Do the asides and the coming forward on the front stage contribute to the movement on stage? Does Quinault's Act I, Scene 3, contribute to movement? Find other scenes that seem static or dynamic, and then make conclusions about the movement on stage in both comedies.

e. *French Color Added to the Action:*
Molière's *Blunderer* could be played anywhere, not only

in Sicily, as stated in the preceding part, page 101. Quinault's *Indiscreet Lover* is played in Paris, or rather in a
Parisian suburb. Since inns in France were on highways,
the names of the inns are taken from actual inns, the
enumeration of meals and drinks is realistically related to
the French *cuisine* of the seventeenth century, and the
reference to the lily flower, an ornament characteristic of the
ancient bearings of the French kings and, in an ironic
manner, for French prisoners condemned to the galleys,[6]
is essentially French. What can you say on the basis of
this feature of French against the Italian situation of the
plays compared? Who seems more original in this regard?

f. *Inspiration vs. Invention:*
    If we accept that both Molière and Quinault have used
    L'Inavvertito as a source of inspiration, where does this
    inspiration seem more concealed?

g. *Positive vs. Negative Vision of the Society:*
    Describe the lovers in both plays. How is the rival pre-
    sented? In *L'Inavvertito*, Cintio, one of the rivals, is a
    scholar; in *The Blunderer*, Leander is a young gentleman
    of good birth (see the list of characters). In both plays
    the author is consistent in portraying them. How con-
    sistent is Quinault? According to the first act what do we
    learn about Lisipe? Compare his confidences to Cleander
    (Act I, Scene 4): "I have worked for a rather long
    time. . . . I didn't gain anything but beating," and his self-
    exaltation toward the end of the first act, in Scene 5: "As
    far as I know, nobody who isn't a descendant from a noble
    and rich family would get her daughter in marriage. I
    assure you . . . this mother will never have another son-
    in-law but myself."

Are the two girls presented as positive types? In the Italian
and in Molière's comedies they are reserved. How is
Lucresse? And how is the blunderer himself, besides being

silly and marring all? Is a gambler a positive type of the
society? Compare.

h. *Dramatic Tension:*
Where is the tension stronger? Compare the situations in
the plays. In Scene 4 of Act II, Philipin is concealed in a
closet and hears how Lisipe speaks about his intention to
come there and how Lucresse admits his presence in the
closet. Find similar scenes of strong dramatic tension in
the plays and make a conclusion about where the suspense
is mostly pathetic.

i. *The Blunderer's Initiation in the Servant's Plans:*
Is the master blunderer equally initiated in the plans of
his sly servant in every play? Compare Act II, Scene 5,
when Philipin tells Lucresse "he wanted to keep the secret
from the sight of his master blunderer," i.e., on purpose.
Is that so in other plays? Don't we have the impression
that both Barbieri and Molière have the tricks disclosed in
front of the master when it is too late, i.e., because of lack
of time to prepare him for the trick? Molière even has the
servant prepare a role with his master to play in his trick,
but not up to the end. Every servant is afraid of having
his plans marred if the master knows all the details of the
trick. What is your conjecture about Quinault's keeping
the trick secret in front of the master blunderer, on purpose?

j. *Laughter Achieved Through Language:*
In Scene 7 of Act II, when Carpalin looks for the pretended letter announcing losses of Lisipe's father and finds
instead a letter to his "late godfather's cousin's nephew's
brother's son," humor is achieved through grammatical
juxtaposition of genitives. What kind of humor is this?
Do we find a similarly innocent humor in the other comedies? What kind of words do the master-and-servant
couples throw at each other when they are angry? Be-

sides, Lisipe's word correction when Carpalin speaks of "puncture," and Lisipe corrects him, using "pleurisy" instead of "puncture," is a characteristic feature of the intelligence both show. Neither really knows what he is talking about. Lisipe just uses the word "pleurisy" for "puncture" (in French, *crevaison,* i.e., exploding or, speaking of a bicycle tire, "puncture"), which seems to him more scientific. Besides, coarse humor is used as well. Thus, a great variety of devices is achieved through words and their juxtaposition more or less belonging to the *savoir vivre.* The maid Rosette's manner of speaking is well pointed out. Her verbs are full of feelings (Scene 1 of Act III). Compare her speaking manner with other females in *The Indiscreet Lover;* aren't they differentiated? Compare them with Molière's women. Philipin likes mockeries, but up to a certain degree. In Act III, Scene 1, he says, "Truce to mockeries." Thus even the same person uses different moods in his/her speaking manner. How is it in the other plays?

k. *Honesty:*

Compare the main characters. Is Philipin honest (Act III, Scene 2)? In Act III, Scene 4, he says to Cleander: "Sir, you have to lie." And Cleander's answer comically emphasizes the opposite: "That's true." The third character present at this time, Lisipe, doubts, is distrustful and takes fright of everything. In this way Quinault has them represent the three main types of society, one being straight, the other foxy-sly, and the third afraid of everything and not daring anything or daring too much out of fear of consequences. Try to find in Molière's play a juxtaposition of some representatives of society, according to his vision. As an example take Scene 1 of Act IV in *The Blunderer.* Instead of "you have to lie," the servant's advice is "play your part in the play perfectly by heart," i.e., also, in other words, a lie. Mascarille is as sly as Philipin. Trufaldin, in Scene 3, is suspicious and makes inquiries; he is abusing Lelio, calling him Mr. Cheat, in Scene 8 of Act IV, after having found out the truth. In comparing these three types juxtaposed by Quinault in one scene, in several other scenes of the same act coming together and unveiling the plot, what could we state in form of a conclusion?

What is the relationship between the concept of honesty, "taking liberties" probably toward the code of ethics of the seventeenth century, and suspicions? See Scene 7 of Act III.

Cleander's conception of honesty changes with his humor. Report on it, basing your opinion on Scene 9 of Act III, when he comes to Lidame after having lost in gambling. Compare Cleander's gambling and its effects on beating with Lelio's honesty

Act III, Scene 3, Cleander boasts about having succeeded in making a good impression of sincerity on Lidame, when he has just played a trick on her. Compare his attitude with Lelio's honesty in saving a purse of Trufaldin, a slave from jail, and his respecting his own word as a pledge to do nothing but wait quietly, to let another work for him (Act V, Scene 5, his monologue), like Barbieri's protagonist.

l. *Parallel Speaking Without Recognition:*
Act IV, Scene 1, offers a comical situation. Rosette and Philipin arrive on stage from two different sides, say the same thing in slightly different words, and perceive each other after having said for seven times that they were going to see each other. Quinault's sense of humor invents this parallel speaking, which is not to be found in Molière's or Barbieri's plays, among a loving couple's dialogues. This parallel speaking is simultaneous; therefore, the lovers don't understand each other, and create a comical speed of words.

m. Clothes:
In Act IV, Scene 7, Lidame traces a picture of French clothes of the time. Can you find such a picturesque description in Molière's *Blunderer?* Can this detail add to the French background of the play?

2. Questions for students in comparative literature, regarding John Dryden's *Sir Martin Mar-All* and his sources:

   a. Was Dryden's comedy originally created as an adaptation of the comedies mentioned before? Whose work was his main source?

   b. The Theme: Is it the same in all three comedies mentioned before and in Dryden's *Sir Martin Mar-All?*

   c. How do the endings vary?

   d. Describe the stratagems in all these comedies and compare them.

   e. Which one of the comedies having a common theme seems most comical and amusing on stage, in reading?

   f. Follow other questions regarding Quinault's comedy in comparing Quinault and Dryden, their vision of the society, and their national color added to the characters, their names, and so on.

NOTES

1. *Molière's Works,* Ernest Rhys, ed., Everyone's Library (New York: Dutton, 1929), vol. I.
2. See Louis Petit de Julleville, *Répertoire du Théâtre Comique en France au Moyen Âge* (Paris, 1886) and *Recueil de farces françaises inédites du XVᵉ siècle* by Gustave Cohen, The Medieval Academy of America (Cambridge, Mass., 1949), among others *La Braggarde;* and the *Monologue du Franc-Archier de Baignolet,* as it appeared in the Copenhague Col-

lection of documents for the History of the Old French Theatre, *Nouveau Recueil de Farces françaises des XVᵉ & XVIᵉ siècles,* according to a document belonging to the Royal Library of Copenhague, edited by Emile Picot and Christophe Nyrop (Paris, 1880)

3. Quotation of John Palmer's *Molière* (New York: Blom, 1970), p. 117.

4. In Act IV, Scene 9, Leander speaks to Mascarille as to a young fellow.

5. See Etienne Gros, *Philippe Quinault. Sa Vie et son oeuvre* (Paris: Aix-en-Provence, 1926)

6. See Note to Act I, Scene 3.